Those Birthdays In-Between

Those Birthdays In-Between

Rene G. Parent

Order this book online at www.trafford.com
or email orders@trafford.com

Most Trafford titles are also available at major online book retailers.

Printed in the United States of America.

ISBN: 978-1-4269-7195-2 (sc)

Trafford rev.06/01/2011

 www.trafford.com

North America & International
toll-free: 1 888 232 4444 (USA & Canada)
phone: 250 383 6864 ♦ fax: 812 355 4082

Dedication

Family, friends, and complete strangers help write a book. Thanks to Trafford for allowing more people to publish their ideas, experiences and adventures. Thanks Ivy, Matt, Ryan and Rosie who call checking in on the writing progress and are no longer strangers.

Other times, events tell the story best. Family and neighborhood events which include celebrating those birthdays in between, especially when reaching decade changing milestones or marked with surprise parties. Bob, yours are first.

And a special thanks to my wife and daughters who travel alongside creating those story moments. It's not so much what you write down, rather what others tell themselves as they read alongside. Still they help edit, suggest front cover design and back cover summary. Writing - a conversation we place ourselves within.

Chapter 1

"We are on the back of the ocean," said Abby. There's no sand in sight. Her postcard day at the coast includes sand - beachfront sand. Instead we overlooked vegetation, two story homes, and the ocean in the distance.

I found a book in Hawaii and fifteen years later find it once again on our Oregon garage floor. My mother in law's postcard falls from this book and is story seed for writing one of my own. I would later place *Twice Found Postcards* on a hotel corridor bookshelf. I take *The Best of Families* and replace it with the book I just wrote on the lives of family including my mother in law and her Maui crescent moon postcard tucked within.

Books are in various stages of being written, printed, and read. Writing continues before breakfast and the prescribed physical therapy exercises. Sometimes we wait until after volunteering with third grade readers. Other times while waiting for kids to cross the street after a day of school, or waiting for a book club to begin.

Writing progresses at its own pace. Janice who sits close by asks if my book is published. "I'm working on it," I tell her. The publishing houses e-mail a similar response. We write of family vacations, twice found postcards and the surprise birthday celebrations in between.

Chapter 2

Madeline's sleepover leaves her with one hour of rest, thus she napped for much of yesterday. I walked back from Starbucks, meeting others along the wooded trail. A sunny day previews spring.

We write in early morning to capture the rhythm of day. Wednesdays, I help my daughter's classmates read in third grade. Reading, a skill which reflects our later life.

We decide the end by what we choose to read. Perhaps America suffers the consequences of Reality Television?

People escape from their everyday reality. It's unemployment for nearly a tenth of our country. We watch as our lifestyle and contributions dissolve.

"We're all in the same boat," goes the familiar refrain. Today, fewer are in positions to help others as they concentrate on keeping their own boat afloat. "Be patient and keep the faith," say the mortgage brokers. Do they relay this message to us, or remind themselves?

Spring is in the air. The birds chirp outside my window. Next week, clocks lose an hour as we spring forward. We in turn hurry our schedule to make up for the lost time. Still the extra light at the end of day is welcomed.

Today my writing waits until the kids are dropped off at school. The dishwasher hums from the kitchen. The washing machine whirls from the laundry, then emptied and ran again.

Similar routine in the garage as I recycle a bit of last week and clean off residue from a passing bird.

The week before I went outside to wash the car. A while back we considered installing a sunroom. It sounded great until the salesman mentions the ongoing rinsing of glass panels. "Just do it while it's raining" he says. "That way you don't have to rinse."

Thus once the downpour started last week, I thought why not wash some of the winter grime from our car. It worked although I got drenched in the process. Still the car is clean until the next storm.

Tonight is a book club at church. Rather than Bible study as usual, we will discuss a recent bestseller which gets people talking. Yesterday our friend in London called. Three hours later we are still discussing books, the writing process and life. "People have choices in what happens to them," she says. I suggest things happen to each of us, life defining events which are out of our control.

I mention I sent my book revisions to the publisher. I mailed them from her hometown zip code. In other words, I went to her parents' neighborhood post office. Tongue in cheek, I wonder if perhaps it will help launch my book. "You did your part," she says. "You wrote it - now there's nothing further one can do to place their book in readers hands."

Thus parts of life are under our control, those life defining moments yet books will do what they will to find their readers. Book clubs often full of debate. Even overseas telephone calls force us to rethink our position. Still I wrote a book and will do what is needed to move it to and from store shelves. While it's not so much what we say, it's what readers tell themselves reading our words; words which we hope resonate.

Writing personal stories by its nature taps into universal themes. We relate to those plots yet sometimes they leave us uncomfortable, vulnerable. We read and somewhere along the way decide we could write a similar tale. The trouble is, our story isn't made up, it happens to us, without our controlling th

outcome. Regardless if people tell us otherwise, our experience speaks a different language. We may all be in the same boat, yet we each relate experiences in our own voice, language, and time.

An airplane climbs in the distance. Birds sing with the advance of spring, the decline in financial markets. We had a book club discussion on a recent bestseller. Our Bible study leader enjoys this particular book as do many Americans, thus the bestseller's list. I ask one of the participants why she thinks it is on readers short list.

"It gets people talking," she replies "although most don't know what they are talking about." She has a degree in Religion and enjoys the book on this basis. Accurate except for one detail, she notes.

I listen wondering just what message clicks with people. Many mention forgiveness and this book allows them to forgive. Each has their own take on the recent bestseller. Books have their own take on life. A popular magazine ranks Portland as an unhappy place. Can this be accurate? The United States must indeed be somber.

Still today this is an easy argument to make. Nearly ten percent are out of work, perhaps more as unemployment reflects those actively searching for work. Book clubs spin another story. We discuss the book and invariably share what concurrently happens in our own lives - lives changed in 2009.

We read about it in newspapers, magazines and even books weave the current state of affairs amid their plots. Fewer are boarding airplanes off to vacation. Spring break is in two weeks. We will take a day trip. For upper middle class, a day trip seems restrictive. We contribute to retirement and 401k plans which in the final analysis require further analysis.

Whether Portland ranks as one of the saddest spots in America is debatable. Would guess there are few places smiling as this year progresses, places and people within those places. Those people who write our story yet have difficulty righting this economic one.

Last night I shared a draft of *A Sibling Within* with Jillian. We are acquaintances as we've sat beside each other since last fall on Tuesday night Bible study. Having a dozen siblings, people give us strange looks initially, then realize we had nothing to do with it. I thought Jillian would enjoy this element of my book, told a sibling at a time.

My family of birth, along with my adoptive family in the Tenderloin hotel front lobby. They too become family. I write about eight of them and mention a few more in the book. One, the wild and crazy woman. Another answers her door scantily dressed. Yet another dances through life, although most watching would say the music had stopped long before. Perhaps this is a formula which gets some through their day.

We write what is currently happening or reflect on days past, gleaning lessons left behind. We write of the people met and those who meet us. Writing a book is one way to meet lots of people at once, yet the better books allow us to meet the author as well.

By the time we are done reading their words we better appreciate the book, often a translation of their life. Read ninety nine percent of fiction begins biographical. "I tell the story of my life over and over," said one writer. We write what we know from where we are. We hope the reader later enjoys our words, even those found in lobbies which later build story. We hope they enjoy reading about themselves or maybe how times were back then, whether at Bible study or volunteering in third grade classrooms.

Chapter 3

Writing takes in the everyday and goes from there. We log in what is seen and heard outside or a room away. Sometimes it's a hotel lobby within San Francisco's Tenderloin district.

Other times it's elementary school children rushing through breakfast. Traffic outside, airplanes overhead, laundry whirling. It all get tossed in. Later in the rewrite, we recognize story threads tucked within.

Writing writes itself if only we get out of the way. Often a story ends elsewhere and not necessarily one of our own. We use our words yet sometimes it is a universal theme. Writing personal accounts hits on humanity without our effort. We write about our books and people we share them with. The best ones include ourselves in the mix. They use our voice, log experience, and reflect our setting.

Today it's back to the telephone store. Our cell phone comes up under a different name on caller ID. My daughter Madeline recently took a call looking for a criminal. Last night someone was busy texting.

I will drive to Gresham and sort this out. May leave with yet a new telephone number. Numbers in our lives, they accumulate along with the recharging cables, accessories to modern life.

Birds sing this morning, yet some panic maybe they returned too early as it's near freezing again this week. We have a birthday party to attend an hour up the interstate. The cousins home is high atop a hill. Another nine year old celebrating his birthday. One of my older brothers also celebrates on March seventh.

Last night I read through *A Sibling Within*. Fun, imagining my friend Jillian reading the same sections. What does she think as she reads through? My book introduces chapters a sibling at a time. I bring in two at a time for six chapters.

Jillian perhaps enjoys this part of the book and meeting folks who people the Tenderloin. I include character sketches of eight, and maybe one hits home with her. They are people who people her world and ours.

Still later I introduce my sister and how those defining events color each day going forward. It's a book about me and my every day experience, even those experiences taken from twenty and thirty five years ago. Realistically, the best books contain a bit of our story within the narrative. Rather than unique or special, they take us in and carry us further.

A story pulls us along if it resonates. Still the bookstores ask, "What makes your book unique or special?" Suppose taking it further, major bookstores insist they carry books which are unique and special.

It may be their hope yet there are only so many storylines. Many lives parallel in the final analysis. It's how we frame stories which separate them. Where we tell the story from, and perhaps not so much what we say.

Still what readers tell themselves matters. We start with words, our story, where they take it is up to them. Thus they have a say in how stories progress. Ideally they follow along through the final chapter. If not, maybe it was the book's intent to take them elsewhere. Fiction does it best, taking a circuitous route, sometimes beginning with the story incoming on cell phones.

We have a new telephone number this morning. We were receiving text messages, and cell phone calls looking for criminals. The Caller ID was wrong. Today we have a new telephone number. Change has been promised, even telephone numbers change.

We are midway through the third month of the year and conditions continue to deteriorate. It's not the message, change envisioned for ourselves or our once prosperous country.

We drive an hour north for a birthday party. Hunter turns nine less than a month from our daughter Abigail. 2000 was a busy year. Now nine years later we watch them grow. "He looks older than me," she remarked last night during dinner.

She looks forward to the school carnival next weekend. Before the school fundraiser, we will meet friends at a local restaurant. Another birthday, a belated birthday party for a mid seventy year old. He will be surprised as we are meeting under the guise of celebrating my wife's birthday.

Lots of birthdays this time of year. There are five birthdays in March in my family of birth. Suppose it meant a birthday cake a week, or maybe they combined celebrations back then. Mine is in September, while the rest of the family birthdays are over by July. I had a season of my own. Still few look forward to turning a year older, in spite of the cake, balloons and celebration.

The furnace shut off. There is no snow on the ground, although forecasted this weekend. Sun breaks hint of spring. After a record snow, many look forward to spring. More light, warmer weather to spend time outside. We turn the clocks forward an hour tomorrow, a welcomed change. While our day doesn't really change, adjusting clocks let us enjoy an extra hour of daylight.

My brother's father in law has a surprise eightieth party this weekend. I wrote a note, holding it until after the birthday party. I received an invitation mailed from an unknown Vermont address. I wondered what might be in this mailing. Fortunately it was a surprise birthday party invitation and nothing more.

We write in early morning of the airplane flying overhead, crinkling writing paper, the shadow of our writing hand. Sometimes we take note, other times too far within thoughts to notice what happens beyond our writing desk.

Today a birthday party calls. Distraction is good as we further this economic uncertainty. "We tread new ground," warn commentators. "Everyone's on their own. It defies explanation," they continue. Still government has penalized the productive in the group.

Driving to the birthday party yesterday, Abby notes there is no snow on the ground as we climb ridges off Interstate 5. "Wait," I tell her. Mid afternoon we have a snow flurry.

Snowflakes the size of thumbnails. Luckily the weather is warm otherwise those size snowflakes would accumulate quickly. Our cousins received five and a half feet during the December storm. They, too, tire of snow.

This morning we have another dusting. Most are ready for spring. Madeline practices her violin. She recently bought a music book; no words nor notes, rather it lets her write her own music. She has the first sentence written and has notes to music down three rows in her otherwise blank music book. "Write what you hear," I tell her. Start where she is and go from there.

Don't stop until she finishes. True for writing words, notes - music. Write what we hear, not so much what is said. Although some say we talk from the page, I think it's more someone overhearing thoughts; our thoughts logged in. Thoughts written down so others can read our words and thoughts behind those words. Sometimes editing, we've forgotten what we wrote, and maybe had help writing those words.

We write daily, although some days this is late morning, after church and eating brunch. Today we turn clocks ahead an hour. Madeline and I turned eleven of them ahead last night. Today Abby has a fever and sleeps in. At 11:50 am she eats breakfast.

Many linger, sleep late this morning. Perhaps running on a similar schedule, yet clocks tell them they run late. Yesterday we walked a local hotel corridor with glassed in bridge overlooking their pool. One side had a cascading water feature. I hadn't noticed it before. "I saw it and assumed you had too," says Madeline. "Otherwise I would have told you," she continues.

We celebrate birthdays for nine year olds. They enjoy their day as they open Lego's. We enjoy the view from their home atop a ridge. Windows frame nature, without subdivisions visible. Snow falls heavily at times amid a surprise snowfall early March. Later we discuss current state of affairs. My wife is asked what I do. She starts with I'm a stay at home dad, an accountant. Later she mentions I've been writing.

This opens conversation. I mention many pencil in stories of their own, furious with the current state of affairs. It's a bonanza for publishers. We leave the birthday party with more readers looking forward to reading our words. It's my hope they get beyond my details and reflect on their own. First we place ourselves at birthday parties and take readers alongside from there.

Chapter 4

It snows this morning. It snowed yesterday. Just now my pen runs out of ink. Can I write it any clearer? Snow and dry ink sum up early spring.

Neighbors were over last night. They visited and dropped off a card for my wife Melissa who turns forty five on Friday the thirteenth. They visit while Abby takes her temperature. She has a flu bug and fever. Madeline and I were at church school. Madeline learns how to make pretzels, those praying bits of dough, better warm with salt. I listen to a group prepare for RCIA, a program which invites people into the Catholic church.

We studied the Nicene Creed. It took several councils to write and written well enough to survive through the years. It's a recap of what we believe, our creed. We believe in the Father, Son and Holy Spirit. Still I know this yet hold Father above the other two. The creed says they are a trinity; three in one God.

We met in the Religious Education director's trailer as it is warmer. A smaller room to heat instead of the normal elementary school classroom. The chairs are more comfortable as well.

Abby sleeps in as snow falls this morning. I will read more in my book *A Sibling Within*. There is a series of steps to writing. Write daily placing words to the page. They form, build our background music. Later we find story seeds. Place them interspersed within the ongoing routine of life. Yesterday's emergency room visit with a friend qualifies as story seed.

There is a story within this hectic experience. Hurried yet it lingers for five hours. There is anticipation, excitement and worry. There are telephone calls, insurance cards and uncertainty. Build around this, say books on writing.

Then reread rough drafts. This is the second edit, which leads to the third. Still we check for punctuation and grammar in early rereading. Be on the lookout for story. It gets better with each edit. Writing, not so much a better plot, rather how story is told - the words used and those left behind.

Continue to write. Later start reading the story to someone in particular. How would they hear our words? I was three quarters through reading to a college friend's mom when our London friend called that her mom was in the emergency room.

She'd driven herself and it is eye trouble, thus it isn't serious, life threatening serious. Still I later join her mom in the emergency room wait area. My plan was to read more of my story. This didn't happen as I drove through hail and snow en route to the hospital. In the distance was clear blue sky.

A strange weather day and this too is thrown in our stories. Today it snows. Mid March and many in the Pacific Northwest tire of the white stuff. We write about it, some days getting a new pen and more ink to log in our whereabouts.

This morning that includes mere frost. Three days now it has hailed or snowed without accumulation. We watch from a window as snowfall brings a sense of quiet hitting the ground. Flakes the size of thumbnails clearly seen as they fall and scatter.

The wind makes a flurry as I walked to the mailbox. Yesterday the year's final financial details were in the mail. Now I can complete tax paperwork for the past year. People suffer losses, yet communities tax those otherwise dismal returns. This is our tax code, go figure.

I will spend much of today filling in pages of tax forms. Federal and then more for the state. Each have programs they hope to fund, or this year, keep afloat. Remember, we are all in the same boat. Abby sleeps in with her lingering fever. Madeline has violin class and wonders if anyone will notice her missing button.

Some will, yet there are more important things than one of eight buttons missing on classmate shirts. Today's style of holes and bleached clothing, few notice a missing button. This may start a trend going forward.

Last night I went to a book club. A group of thirteen discussed a recent bestseller. Some add they know the author, others recently heard him speak. Still others note he is unpretentious, having to purchase a new pair of jeans while in New York on book tour.

I sat quietly as the group couldn't understand people who didn't get this book. It's that good. I sat wondering how the group leader must feel.

She introduced the book to our Bible study group weeks before. I later asked what worked for her in this book. Still I finished writing one I've been in the process of writing for some time. Book clubs, as good as any place to catch a line of dialogue.

We write of mid March snow, the book clubs which embrace an author, or not. We hear overhead airplanes while planning the remainder of the day; bills, accounts to review and e-mails to anticipate.

Yesterday the publisher e-mailed they wanted two lines sent to them via e-mail. They are not the first to suggest my penmanship illegible. Still they didn't ask for better words. What happens in our day fills our pages. Sometimes we stop in at book clubs to learn. The book doesn't do it for us, still people relating their experiences may include a story seed or something we can take away. The book not so much, perhaps the reviewers have something noteworthy to add.

We remain silent as they continue their insight. Like the economy, we are each on our own page, learning as we go, adjusting steps and words as we go forward.

Today begins off schedule. Abby is in bed coughing. A week later she still fights a fever. Madeline is on her lollygagging routine.

Up late, then a leisurely breakfast. I've since put the recyclables away, and opened the garage. The car is now in the driveway and still no Madeline.

I'm in a bit of a hurry. My routine stopped. Melissa is home to take Abby to the doctor later this morning. She's online in the den. I want my morning writing done before heading out the door. Instead I wait for Madeline to hurry along. She joins me, one shoe on, one off. We drive to school and I stop by the office letting them know Abby will be out sick again today.

I quickly search the lobby for Marilyn. She took a copy of *A Sibling Within* the last time we met. I wondered how she liked it, or even whether she liked it. Walking out of the school I pass Marilyn in her red Cherokee sport utility vehicle. "I'll be right back," she says. "Let me drop off my granddaughter."

We sit in the car as it's barely above freezing this morning. "I loved it," she says. "I read it twice as I didn't connect early on. Later it all went together and I really enjoyed it. It made me reflect on my own life," she continues. I thank her. Again, I thank her as she says what authors hope to hear. It's not so much what we write, rather readers take something away after spending time, with our books, our words - us.

She enjoys the walking trail descriptions and the everyday routine. The part with Wallowa Lake without my mother in law gets to her, as does my seeing that red truck from the early 1960's. Now blocks away, it helps me write my second book, *A Sibling Within*. The book made her realize she too has siblings within, although she is an only child. "There's no way," I tell her she is without siblings in this world.

Still this is a rhetorical question for each of us. How can a Tenderloin district exist amid prosperous America?

Yesterday I learned a tenant passed away. He lived in the same apartment for twenty nine years, twenty since I've owned the apartment building. It's been subsidized living for those years, meaning below market rent. We do what we can in this world.

Still I was taken aback when they asked to remove appliances. Not washer and dryer, instead the kitchen appliances. I always wondered if I'd get a thank you, or some serendipitous reward for housing people. Helping them with lower rents so perhaps they can enjoy a bit more life.

Today Marilyn gives me this thank you. She enjoys my book. It makes her reflect on her own life. Perhaps "listen" as she phrases it. Some days go like this, people appreciate those things we aren't sure what we do as we set out doing them. Writing for example. Even the writing began off schedule. We fill in later.

Mrs. Onstott's receipt sits on my desk. Outdoor school for sixth grade students is a month away. A sleep over at the beach, they get a lesson on being away from home. There will be physical exercises as well as learning about marine life.

Madeline asks if they'll have to go on those early morning walks. "This is optional," my wife says. She's just returned from an hour long briefing on the sixth grade students upcoming adventure.

Bring sleeping bags, lots of socks, and label everything. I saw the ocean at age eighteen and having a sixth grade trip to the coast seems a luxury. Realistically, it helps them everyday going forward. Doubt there are Oregonian classmates who haven't seen the coast. Oregon the place with airplanes flying overhead and Cascade peaks looming in the distance. Oregon with its renowned coastline and desert two hours inland, cutting through the central part of the state.

Orchards, forests, and rain paint our state, the one celebrating its one hundred fiftieth birthday this year. We are just atop California. "Oregon is for dreamers," waves the current state marketing banner, even if some surveys rank us unhappy.

The recyclables are curbside. It's barely twenty degrees outside. This weekend is Carnival at elementary school - fun and games amid a fundraiser. Madeline volunteers to help, she runs a student store this morning.

She's been awaken twice and says she is getting ready. Still I don't hear movement from that part of the house. Abby sleeps in day six of a flu which has kept her close to home. She coughs amid battling fevers. She missed yesterday's field trip to downtown Portland. She's missed yet another week of school. I hope her immunities build.

We write in early morning. Yesterday I spent time finding the front cover picture for *A Sibling Within*. Marilyn at the elementary school says to go with a montage, my sister at center with the Tenderloin group forming a circle. I later see a photograph of an airplane on Abby's digital camera.

I'll go with this view of an airplane window looking out upon sky, clouds in that sky. My book's subtitle could read "Still we take them with us, or maybe they take us along." Just now a small airplane makes its way across our neighborhood; a small, loud airplane which perhaps flies too low. We write what goes on pages and happens outside our windows.

Today is laundry and errands. Mid March and the new year progresses. This weekend is a brunch for my father who turns eighty eight. They celebrate in Vermont. I e-mail we won't make it. Realistically we won't make my nephew's wedding later in July, something about the economy.

We write about it. It lingers on people's minds. Still the celebrations continue. Saturday we will have breakfast with friends. My wife too turns a birthday calendar page on Friday the thirteenth. We'll see how this goes.

I read through a draft of *Twice Found Postcards*. It recaps having breakfast a month ago as a postcard hovers over our breakfast table. This imaginary postcard fills a book with storyline. Madeline learns of watermelon seeds and how they are analogous to writing, keep the seeds, build on story seed.

She just finished a telephone call earlier with our friend in London. She called to wish my wife a happy birthday. They were college roommates many years before. This too is an important part of the college experience. Ideally lifelong friendships are formed. Regrettably too often we connect at the holidays, birthdays, or consider them as we edit.

Abby sleeps in. It's been a week of flu for her. No school and not much activity other than sleeping in. She missed her classmates walking tour of downtown Portland. Madeline did a similar tour, returning with the mayor's business card. She toured city hall among other downtown points of interest.

Barely thirty degrees this morning and many wish spring would get here. It would be nice to turn down the furnace and spend more time outside. We had record snow, maybe this will be a record summer filled with weeks of sunshine. A few cards have come in the mail. Madeline made one of her own. Abby bought one which plays music.

We will have a party later tonight, with pizza followed by birthday cake. Tomorrow a breakfast across town before the elementary school bazaar. Yesterday morning I read through the remainder of *A Sibling Within*. Later I input a few revisions and reprinted a dozen pages.

Short the dedication, that book is done. I mailed my first one late September. Six weeks and the book would be printed. Mid March and still I wait. I wanted the first copy done before sending a second book to this publisher. I will call next week. Wonder what timeframe they tell writers these days. Six weeks clearly didn't happen on the first book. Let's hope they are more prompt with the second.

I wanted it available for Christmas. That didn't happen. Maybe this second one will make the holiday shopping season this year. Condensing books to a dozen key words is difficult.

They recommend eliminating the broad, general subjects, such as life, death, and God. Instead use search words like career, relocation and prayer. Still to condense two hundred pages into merely a few words or categories is difficult. We hope to choose the right ones for those browsing online for reading material

Madeline is unusually quiet in the kitchen. I'd better check on her. The school bazaar starts in fifteen minutes. We write of today and those days which came before. This morning we are going to breakfast across town with friends and the birthday girl.

My wife celebrated a birthday yesterday. Today we will surprise friends with a birthday gift as the husband recently had a birthday of his own.

Last night we had pizza, cake and opened gifts. Later the telephone rang. Caller ID says it's a call from Connecticut yet it is an older sister in Vermont on the line. Abby speaks to her for awhile. Her Flat Sally grade school project makes it to Vermont, however its hand falls off en-route.

Madeline sent one years before. She says her classmates had a hard time with the maple syrup candy. It's an acquired taste. Later my sister from Connecticut is on the telephone line.

"Read *The Lottery*," she says. She thinks it takes place near our area, the Puget Sound area. "The humor is much like ours. Read it," she urges. She'd also said this about a recent bestseller; a book I find dark, yet enlightening enough to finish writing one of my own.

Then my brother from Philadelphia is on the telephone. We talk of his drive up to New England. Delays in New York City, although nice weather along the route. Pavement in Vermont is what to expect at winter's end.

They are in town for my father's eighty eighth. He too has a birthday on Friday the thirteenth. Like my wife, thirteen has been a lucky number for him. Most bet on other digits.

Abby finally gets rid of a week long flu. I input more pages of the draft to *Twice Found Postcards*. It recounts some of my mother in law's life. More on the lives she influenced, and left behind in her trail of smoke.

It's a book quickly written. It falls into place, although we still spend time writing, editing and inputting our words on the computer. Perhaps this book formatted itself quicker than others. There is order, it clicks early on. We did.

My friend who volunteers on Wednesdays read through *A Sibling Within*. She loved it. Her tears yet it wasn't so much my words, rather what those words meant - what readers tell themselves reading along.

There's no better experience than have someone enjoy our written words. "Why don't you write about family" she now asks. "Write about them." I'm not sure how to frame this book, frame that story. What exactly do she and others want to hear?

The details and physical descriptions of my family? The daily routine of a dozen siblings? How life plays out for each of us? Marilyn is an only child and suppose any detail on siblings interests her.

It is foreign to her, no matter how we tell it. Where we start or end isn't so important. Most stories start in the middle; in the middle of writing, in the middle of families, in the middle of car front seats.

I thought about writing on family. I'd sit inside our new 1968 Buick. The new car scent captures my imagination, newness in the Buick LeSabre air.

Yesterday we met friends for breakfast. They were late to the restaurant. While waiting a couple pass by our table. Melissa worked with this woman many years and we've exchanged birthday and holiday cards ongoing.

She and her husband stop to visit. We pick up where we left off, although it's been five years since meeting face to face. "It's not that we don't think about you," she says. They haven't aged a day, while they look at our nine and eleven year olds. It made our breakfast, before we meet up with expected company. They show up later, gift in hand.

We return for the school Carnival, a few hours of fun activity for kids, young and old. Madeline and others of her sixth grade class volunteer. We said goodbye to Melissa's former co-worker. They recently had a car accident and now she and her husband shop for a used Toyota, a Rav-4 like the one my wife drives. They even drive our vehicles, I think to myself. Some people we meet and bond with quickly.

My sister recommended a book while we talked on the telephone two days ago. It's called *The Lottery*. A book written by Patricia Wood. I google it and read a summary. It includes a grandmother, a mentally challenged grandson and a lottery win. Life, death and relationship is also there.

Meeting my mother in law was an early gift. She was a dynamic person, although she too went by Patricia Wood, however short lived this name change. We adjust ongoing. Still those who pass us in this life, influence ongoing, they never leave our side. Memories keep them alive. They often are those who've mentored, yet it takes years to reflect on the gift they leave behind. We include them in conversations going forward.

Yesterday the obituary of a twenty year tenant was in our newspaper. Mid eighty years old, it says he was from the Midwest, a musician. Simple enough yet we understand he played music.

"A house without a piano isn't home," he once said. "It lacks something." Suppose he meant more than simply music, rather moments, memories. A life of moments, memories - music. A home filled with music and not merely a song at birthday celebrations.

Today it rains, a downpour which may awaken early spring vegetation. Already the heather blooms. Now grass will spring back to its vibrant green. I spent part of yesterday searching for places to spend spring break. It's here in one week. Maui is available, for a price. Phoenix has many options. Savannah surprised me being double the cost of a Hawaiian vacation. My niece studies in this resort town.

Rosarios Resort on Orcas Island in the Washington state San Juan Islands is full. Today it might be cheaper to drive rather than deal with flights and airport parking fees. Later I look at Harrah's in Lake Tahoe. They too have availability in this recession.

We may drive there for a change of scene. It's as good as any spot to write. It has been an eventful location in my life, a front row seat on several occasions. My first time on snow skis, marriage and now writing on life, a family of lives celebrating those birthdays in between.

Chapter 5

Finding parking downtown Portland is a challenge, even on Sundays. Yesterday I parked next to a bumper sticker. There was a car underneath, although much of it covered in bumper stickers. Political ones covered the car along with stickers on literacy. "All kids are writers," states one.

There is a writers conference at the downtown library. I walked the few blocks there after finding parking. Later I walk The Esplanade, an hour long path around the city. It allows us to walk along the downtown park and across the Steel Bridge. Then walk a series of floating walkways which overlook the downtown core from across the Willamette River. Then it's back across the Hawthorne Bridge.

I took a leisurely pace, although there are joggers and bikers alongside. Wind and rain interspersed with sun breaks color my walk. Earlier I met a few publishers, printers, editors and others ready to help move books along. Many had business cards or up coming meetings to further a conversation.

Some sell their books. Others tell how far along they are in the process, either midway writing or looking for a sales lead. Most agree they prefer to write and leave marketing, the sales to others. Still writers must do the leg work to move their books. Early on we write and then spend an equal amount of time promoting our books, words - us.

Suppose it helps if we are committed to our books. Writing requires commitment. I read a book recently which says all stories require commitment; a commitment to stay with the process long enough to tell the story.

Today we not only must tell a good story, we must follow through making this story, our book, available to the buying public. Whether there are sales or not, writing is in the doing. Not so much rewarded by later sales or lack of sales. All art is in doing, whether we are rewarded later by frequent sales of our product. Having one person enjoy our work is reward enough. Still this first person is the story's first reader - us.

We write daily of the everyday. Someone asked what I write about at yesterday's library meeting. "Poetry? Fiction?" they ask. I find the person aggressive, this person with the black t-shirt which reads "Write" across the front. Just now it occurs to me who might drive that series of bumper stickers.

I tell him I write words, books of words. I am taken off guard, pressured to reveal what I write, or even if I write. I thought I was off to a writers lecture series. Instead I walk into a series of people peddling their wares, words, themselves. Soon I would join them. Perhaps I already had since I looked forward to this mid Sunday afternoon meeting in the downtown library.

A Starbucks gift card later, I sit in a local grocery store food court and reward myself for the long walk earlier along Portland's waterfront. I enjoy my cup of coffee as I reflect on the writers seminar. I come home with an armful of memos, newsletters, business cards, and contacts. All in all, worth finding a parking spot.

My sister e-mails a recap of the past weekend festivities. There were forty eight at my father's brunch. They roasted his eighty eight years. The weather cooperates and fun for all, including the locally owned and operated hotel. Business booms or at least it did this past Sunday.

Meanwhile Oregon is now in double digit unemployment. Perhaps this explains the tax bills. Four thousand per property, more for income tax. Oregon collects as our state celebrates its one hundred fiftieth birthday this year. States too, commemorate the birthdays in between.

Nationally the numbers aren't much better. Regardless of the rhetoric and special guests on television networks. Invariably they peddle some of their own work. It happens. Marketing keeps us afloat. While it's an interesting college course, marketing is here to stay. It's what moves product.

Marketing tells what we need. I just used an iPod as an example in relating to the kids how marketing works. We must advertise business. Stores advertise, sending coupons and ten dollar rebate checks. Most retailers spend to make others spend.

I mention to the kids marketing builds a need. Suddenly we need something merely a want and clearly not a need, a necessity. Water, food, clothing and shelter are needs. There is no need to market the basics in life. An iPod and next year's hot gadget on the other hand, pure genius, marketing genius.

Marketing invites us to purchase and belong to a club. Wii advertises they bring music into people's lives. I watch thinking a musical instrument might work; place a guitar in your hand. Choose an instrument, just make sure it plays music.

We live in a marketing world. Marketing moves merchandise and books. It's been awhile since the best written book sold. Rather today we are inundated with best selling books; books aggressively marketed. Either the author is a guest on television or their book gets the stand alone rack; one we stub toes upon entering the front door of major bookstores.

The coveted corner atop the heap at Costco or some other mass marketer works too. It's what sells. America does a fine job selling its products, or maybe not so much. Today there is less American made on the shelves.

Even with clever marketing gimmicks Detroit has a hard time convincing Americans to buy American made vehicles. Cadillac requires a double take; they've lost their signature. Mercedes is no longer the stand alone brand they once were. When the world drives luxury, there is something wrong with this picture.

Marketing has us believe everyone is successful. In the meantime, consume; consumption equates to success.

This morning the kids sleep in a few more minutes. Birds sing as the coffeepot echoes from the kitchen. I volunteer later in Abby's third grade classroom. Nine were out sick last week, Abby included. She missed the walking tour of downtown.

Yesterday was a trip to Fedex Office. Tax forms to copy, collect and later file. The news from Washington continues to trouble congress, although they give the bailout money.

Now AIG, once the world's largest insurance company, gives million dollar bonuses. Rather it is us, the collective taxpayer which is the United States government. We now own the majority of this particular company. Government becoming a corporate owner, not so much a watch dog to American business.

News reports feature special guests, experts, and the pundits. Some claim to not being financially literate yet weather this storm with their conservative holdings. We listen to chatter and the collective gab fest.

Today we will read in third grade. Last week we read of war along with a swear word. It makes me wonder why those books are selected. Then again, kids watch television which leaves it wide open, or more apt, closes down their world all the sooner.

It takes away their initiative, talent and energy. There's a reason its called couch potato. Soon the couch becomes inseparable from its occupant. The potato analogy might later match an under utilized brain; passively watching channels, as life passes by.

Remotes keep us in control, as do the intermittent commercials which promise health, wealth or enhancing lives in some way. Disney was featured last night. The internet too, has bargains. Friday two days from now starts spring break, the annual weeklong break from school.

Today's economy keeps many close to home and thus the hotel bargains. The airfare bargains. The vacation packages there for the taking. Some prefer staying close to home as this recession lingers. We watch as they bail out companies; companies with an apparent mission of their own.

We write in early morning of our everyday and those days which don't add up. Still the publishers have a backlog. Many place their thoughts to the page, righting their world, one word at a time noting traffic, birds or tap of a cereal bowl rooms away.

Madeline has her report on Europe today. They entice the principal to see Europe via their travel agency spiel. She practiced several times last night as she points out the Eiffel Tower, the Natschmarket and Salzburg castle. Today is the last day of school before spring break. Abby has a class party. The elementary school has hat day. Odd is better on crazy hat day.

I'll make online reservations in Lake Tahoe for three nights. The rest of the trip will fill on its own. We considered the beach, Bend and Hawaii. Lots of availability as many stay closer to home this spring break.

Madeline just stopped in to see how I liked her hat. Abby is barely out of bed and pours her cereal. Earlier Madeline and I ate a breakfast of eggs, English muffins and orange juice.

"Do Japanese eat eggs?" she asks. I hear, "Do pandas eat eggs?" It's early morning and some don't listen well, or maybe others mumble early on. Let's hope she has more enthusiasm for her RU Lost Travel Agency spiel.

Yesterday I typed more of *Twice Found Postcards*. I read through the beginning pages. Stories are told, building hooks and twists along the way. Marilyn was in the school lobby waiting to volunteer.

We visited awhile before recording the progress of third grade readers. Once a cold read, then a second time to see how they improve. All do better in their second read, the warm read.

Later a group read further in *F - is For Freedom*. One read at a fast pace, skipping whole sentences. She becomes angry and reluctant admitting she missed a few words, lines of words - sentences. She is a fast reader yet there is something to accuracy; this too is noted on their reading progress charts.

Madeline chirps like an owl, surprising herself as she makes this sound. Later she wants help placing her poster board into a plastic bag. It's sprinkling outside so the plastic wrap will protect her report.

I will see AAA later for a trip tik and booklets on Oregon, California, and Nevada. They list routes, and have discounts for hotels along those routes.

Often it seems we are away much longer than mere days. I hope our trip to Lake Tahoe is memorable. We drove there years ago. Our route was deep snow with little traffic, the one recommended by AAA. This time we will stop in Sacramento. Staying on more heavily traveled highways might be a safer bet this time of year.

Madeline practices her report in the dining room. Abby listens. I'll finish writing up this page then shuttle them to school. Just now she mentions the rock church built in 1952 in Finland; it's built underground, made entirely of stone.

There is much to see in Europe. Today this trip abroad is not feasible for many Americans, let alone spend upon landing. Instead it's a road trip to Lake Tahoe. Spring break begins at three pm.

Chapter 6

Yesterday the car shivered. Our Passat wagon reliable for nearly four years, yet a day ago warning lights blinked as the car shook. We leave late for school. Later we walk with violin, Europe report and full backpacks to school down the street. It is also crazy hat day.

I had a crazy day, one which didn't go according to schedule. Days before vacation and the car acts up. I call the Volkswagen dealership. While waiting for the repair, they give complimentary tickets for MAX, the light rail. I take it to the Lloyd Center mall, thinking I will have lunch with my wife, and perhaps leave with her car to pick up the kids from school.

She calls they are celebrating a birthday by going out to lunch. I join them as I know the group well. My wife has worked with many of this group for nearly twenty years. Later the car is fixed, warranty issues and other minor repairs. This is a relief, still we will use my wife's vehicle to drive to Lake Tahoe. Last night I made a hotel reservation along the route. The end of the trip is left open, depending on how much of a hurry we are in returning home. Still weather could be a factor.

Madeline's travel agency report on Europe goes well. Abby comes home with a colorful whirly wheel. They are both excited for the spring break road trip. Lake Tahoe will add to our heart map, those family stories which survive and are relived in telling them.

It's nearly fifty degrees outside, a break before the cold rains return. The yards begin to come alive with green lawns, crocuses, heather and other vegetation either budding or starting to bloom. Spring a beautiful time of year, true most everywhere.

The light rail was standing room only midday yesterday. It's great public transportation is used. During breakfast Madeline asked if people in Japan eat eggs. I thought she asked whether pandas eat eggs.

She walked to the car yesterday afternoon with her friend Maddie. Maddie has a t-shirt with a panda on the front. Wonder if she had a matching hat for crazy hat day. The car shook as I started it yesterday. We will let it rest in the garage while we visit Lake Tahoe this spring break, a gorgeous spot regardless of season.

I put my pen away thinking three pages are written. Only two have writing on them so I'll write more. It's time to get out of town, off routine so we will have more to log in. My wife needs a break from work. The kids will enjoy a break from school. Travel gives us this break.

Vacations present new territory, people and ideas. Ideally we return with a new focus - perspective. We leave our every day routine and return refreshed, ready to pick up where we left off or start anew.

Spring a time to spend outside. Yesterday I walked to the school. The day before I walked around the neighborhood. It'd been a season since walking this route. The wet and often cold weather has kept many indoors for two or three months.

It's nice to finally get more exercise. The coffee shop was full earlier in the week. Wonder if sales have a corresponding drop with the increase in daily sun. Anchorage at one point had the highest concentration of Starbucks. No doubt their sales are higher in winter. We are off to the winter wonderland of Lake Tahoe. First, neighbors will stop for pizza and board games later tonight. Tomorrow we will pack the car.

A load of laundry runs. The suitcases are almost packed. The kids sleep a bit longer. We drive to California today. Spring break, a time to shift routine, take a break from work, study and the every day. Reno offers thirty dollar hotel rooms. They realize people will linger in their restaurants, gift shops if not gamble in their casinos.

The coffee brews from the kitchen. We will drive five to six hours, with a shorter stretch tomorrow. Roads we seldom drive. AAA had many brochures, maps and travel suggestions available.

They also have telephone numbers by state for driving conditions. Snow in Tahoe is a given, still there can be plenty of sunshine along with this snow. I learned to ski at Heavenly in 1977. Later we've visited the area on a few occasions. I hope we will drive its loop around the lake again on this trip. There are wonderful homes lining this route, each with their own Sierra Nevada view.

Last night we played Farkle and discussed starting a business. Our friends are now in their ninth month of business and hit their stride. Life doesn't get more exciting. Money comes in, yet the intangible part keeps the conversation alive, and business afloat.

It's this part which is impetus for many to set off on their own. Entrepreneurs ready to call the shots for themselves, work for themselves. They wonder how things are going for us. I mention my book which was promised six weeks from the end of September. It's a long process placing words in book form. Still moving our books off the bookstore shelves is equal challenge.

We play Farkle. Some rolls of dice luckier than others. So too with life, sometimes it gels, other times not so much. We will drive to Lake Tahoe stopping in Reno and later Sacramento. It is fun getting away. Wonder if many will be on the road, or have people settled in close to home.

End of the third month of the year approaches and little change thus far. Scandal continues, senators take back their position, even word. They don't quite know where they stand. In hindsight, they question their own motives. The public in an uproar regarding the latest round of corporate bonuses paid.

Taxpayer money doing what it does. Thus people set out on their own, having more say in how funds are allocated, or how their time is spent generating income. How their time is spent helping others conduct business. The better businesses conduct their own. They connect with the people being served.

Snow covers vehicles in the hotel parking lot. We stopped overnight in Weed, California on our way to Reno. Reno, a stopover on our way to Lake Tahoe. We see snow during this spring break. Yesterday there were clear skies for much of the route. Rain, heavy rain as we later pull into the hotel lot.

There was a noticeable greener landscape as we drove south. Animals: lambs, goats, cows and horses line the route. Llamas are also there grazing in the nearby fields. Some houses built long before the interstate system became part of their daily view. We drive rolling hills and mountain passes before seeing the "Welcome to California" highway sign.

We stop at the roadside check point. No fruits, vegetables nor plants, so allowed to drive further. I mention to the kids airplanes are washed upon landing in Hawaii. They don't risk contamination to their crops and vegetation. California takes a similar stand monitoring highway traffic.

A few hotel guests get an early start, otherwise the parking lot remains filled with cars and their cover of snow. The hotel offers a breakfast of waffles, danishes, breads, muffins and coffee. Juice and fruit are also available.

Television in the background gives weather updates and late breaking news from Washington. The latest on AIG and two congressmen who have difficulty locating their primary residence. Both select their Maryland home to avoid paying more tax.

Both are later requested to adjust their tax statements. Politicians doing what they do. Some think they are above the law, or law doesn't apply to them. So it goes in Washington.

So too for the weather. Today it snows at the Oregon, California border. High in the Siskyoo Mountains, it probably snows here too often. "Black ice makes driving hazardous," warns the front desk clerk. "I've been here six years," she tells guest in the hotel front lobby.

Birds sing outside the hotel window. Overheard conversation passes through the hall. Interstate 5 is in the distance. There's a knock on the door. The kids and mom are back from breakfast.

They agree there is variety at the self serve breakfast. "This coffee is hot," Abby warns handing it to me. Mom suggests Abby needs pony tails. Madeline thinks I should get another coffee for the road.

"Your contact lens case and solution are still on the counter," my wife reminds me. Packing for an overnight requires repacking in the morning, including the contact lens solution, suitcases and the hot coffee.

Abby sings as her hot chocolate kicks in. So too for her coughs. She is at the end of a week of flu. It's time to place everything back in the sport utility vehicle and drive to Reno on a highway which forgoes the highest passes along the Sierra Nevadas.

The bags are packed. Hotel keys are on the shelf. Abby looks for her drink and stretches the luggage handle. "If you see anything else - just pack it up," she offers as the door slams shut. Time to hit the road.

"Say something newer," says my daughter Madeline. Meanwhile people mingle in the casino lobby. We have an early morning breakfast buffet at Silver Legacy Casino. Reno doesn't have a cloud outside. Winners are inside.

Winners and whiners. A loud slot machine continues to pay. Ongoing the slot machine blares from across the plastic lattice and floral arrangements which line our courtyard breakfast nook. Food is plentiful. The powdered eggs a miss. Fruit directly out of a can feed the masses.

The desserts are heavenly: cheese cake, carrot cake, and coffee breads. After lingering over juice and coffee, they walk over to Circus Circus to catch one of the shows. Jugglers or unicycle riders, maybe jugglers atop those unicycles. Unfortunately the next show begins at five this afternoon.

We will drive over the snow covered rim of mountains encircling Reno on to Lake Tahoe. We will spend four days there this spring break. Last night I left the blackjack table with forty two dollars. It's a thrill to cash out, as it's been a long time since leaving ahead, this time forty two dollars and fifty cents ahead.

A Federal Express truck passes outside the window. An eight by five window if Madeline's foot measurements are accurate. She measures as we debate its size. It's a picture window regardless its exact dimensions. Earlier Madeline spotted school buses from the twenty fourth floor glass wall. We woke up to a helicopter flying mid window. Last night snow flakes floated just outside the window pane.

There is a white dusting on the surrounding mountain range. Downtown blinked with casino lights throughout the evening. Green spot lights lit up the hotel, and our hotel room. Reno continues business this morning outside our window and down the elevator. There are a few conventions in town. A military seminar includes a group from Virginia.

Madeline spots a Bennington, Vermont luggage tag while we wait to check in. The line is twenty people long waiting for one of twenty five hundred hotel rooms. Many with views. Some accept their offer of free champagne. This makes the slow check in more tolerable. Later they ask if we want another drink as we play casino tables.

There are a few blackjacks. There are as many admonishes from fellow gamblers. "The dealer had sixteen," says an older oriental woman. "Always take a hit on fourteen. What are you thinking,?" says another.

My pockets fill with five dollar tokens is what I am thinking. It's a good thought. It is saying something newer.

Winning is more fun. The opulence of casinos tell who wins long term. Still they give away the hotel room, this morning's breakfast and last night's dinner. Reno a favorite stop and a picturesque landscape. Lake Tahoe is just over an hour drive.

We will see what memories Lake Tahoe holds this time. Five years ago, we walked through heavy snow in search of a restaurant. Applebees proved much further down the block than expected.

Chapter 7

The sun makes its way over mountains lighting up Lake Tahoe. It is blue once again with interspersed white along its surrounding mountain slopes. A blue sky covers all as a single jet passes far above.

Checking into Reno's Silver Legacy had a backlog of people; people in town to gamble, shop or relax in the spa. Others see the shows, or sights in and around Reno.

Last night two Tahoe gamblers were heading back to Reno, staying at the Circus Circus before catching a flight back east. They played the blackjack table last night, keeping the dealer and us entertained. They kept the bartender busy too. Later they would drive to Reno in search of the affordable and close to airport hotel room.

A day earlier the hotel provided free champagne for those waiting to check in. "Have one for the road as long as you aren't driving," they offer. So it goes in the Nevada desert, snow on top.

Another airplane makes its way across the clear morning sky. Lake Tahoe, a mirror of deep blue. The hotel room fan the only other sound this morning. We will have brunch at Harrah's later.

The hamburger at Hard Rock Café took two efforts to grill. The first being raw for much of the middle of an otherwise great hamburger. We get extra fries with the replacement. It's five dollars for the beer on tap.

Instead I sample a bottle of Logerstein, New Zealand's brand of beer. Not bad, although much of it sprays upon opening the bottle returning from the grocery store. It must have been a shake filled trip from the parking structure.

I watch as people ask for another card, or are resigned with their numbers. Some staying at thirteen, others doubling down on nineteen. The extra card makes them go over twenty one. Not so nice on the part of the dealer. They might have an obligation to help the blackjack player along.

Still the casino invariably wins as their opulence attests. They may give away rooms, even meals, yet at the end of the day, the house is ahead. So too for the two heading back east today. They were behind yesterday, yet ahead for the week. They didn't mention shows, skiing or other sights. They perhaps never left the casino once the car was parked.

Lake Tahoe glistens blocks away. A few birds fly, otherwise a morning is still in the process of awakening. So too for kids adjusting to the mountain air. It's dry here for some anyhow as we log in more of our spring break. A seagull just flew by feet away from our tenth floor window - a ten by ten window. I measure this time.

This morning there is cloud cover. We will walk to breakfast once everyone is awake. They were up late watching television. I spent much of last night playing blackjack. Hours later I broke even as the dealer shocked himself with a twenty one. Some dealers are more people persons than others.

This one is Hawaiian with a seriousness to his deals. He wins - often. Our table had been on a roll before he came along. The previous dealer was from Brooklyn. Earlier we went to a local restaurant for dinner, then drove a few slopes of the surrounding neighborhood. Lots of lodge style homes, some with lake view, all with snow cover.

The crowds haven't stopped coming to Lake Tahoe. A timeshare salesperson says much the same. Originally from Australia, this is her place in the sun. She traveled the world via a cruise ship career and has seen much to compare. Still Tahoe remains her place in the sun, even years later.

The gambling tables are full mid week. The buffet lines are short, which is a good thing. Requesting we wait forty five minutes or more for guests to serve themselves didn't work in Las Vegas. Lake Tahoe a whole other setting, much more than a mere physical, natural landscape change.

I'm in the conference center logging in more of our week in the Sierra Nevada's. Today we may drive the perimeter of the lake. Yesterday was clear blue skies yet the kids preferred to stay poolside at the hotel.

They swim for an hour and a half. I walk some of the nearby neighborhood. It's thrilling to see La Bella motel thirty years later. Perhaps the small family run motel is now used for longer term tenants. It is worn down, although blocks away from the lake and casinos.

I'd stayed there Christmas 1977. I'd gone to Lake Tahoe without reservation. The owners of this motel, Al and Terry, took me in and let me sleep in their lobby. Later they show me their Tahoe. They too had found paradise. They know many locals and help set the stage to a full holiday week.

This is one New Years I'll never forget. Lake Tahoe, casinos, skiing and buffets is backdrop. I learned to ski that week even though most assume Vermonters already know how. We grow up on skis? The lucky ones do.

We write in hotel corridors, overhearing activity rooms away. A chapel is at the end of the hall. A wealth seminar planned for later today across this hall. Down further someone explains expansion plans, more hotel rooms, slot machines - business.

Two skiers just walked by. Their snowsuits swish as they walk. One card player commented last night it is the first time she has been hot while skiing. Like the rest of us, skiing is usually a cold, freezing experience.

Still in early spring Tahoe sun, skiing is a memorable experience. We phrase it as being hot. I asked her to repeat herself as I heard "caught." Had she been stranded by a patch of bare trail.

"Nice office," comments a repair person as he walks by. "Two phones even," as he continues to move further down the corridor. I look over seeing one. I turn around fully and there is a second telephone just above my head. Last night it was a waitress' tray which hovered above. She stopped by our blackjack table and hits me mid neck.

Later she drops by and spills over the dealer, his dealing apparatus and part of his chair. We joke we need meet this server cross armed, protecting ourselves from her clumsiness. Still she is having a bad day and perhaps fortunate not playing slots or the card tables.

People mill through the hotel. "Hello," some say while others chat on cell phones oblivious to the people around them. Yesterday Abby called wondering where I was. "I am at the hotel front door," I tell her.

She thinks it's our hotel, I am pressing the door bell at La Bella motel. No one answers and there are a few apartment doors open. Lots of bicycles, dogs and furnishings about. Thus it may no longer rent rooms by the night. Terry was an artist and often showcased her natural landscape paintings within the motel.

They are a good memory of Lake Tahoe. Learning to ski is another. For some a timeshare at the base of Heavenly gondola is as good as it gets.

Sunshine works for most of us. Sun, snow and blues of the lake blocks away. It's a postcard setting. Winning at slot machines or the card tables hold special memories. Skiing, hot skiing does it for others.

Lake Tahoe shines outside the window. Evergreens line its shore. Snowcapped mountain peaks in the distance and to the right a nearby mesa. Last night the sun set as we rounded those bends at Zephyr Cove. Melissa took a few pictures, later the kids try capturing a few shots of their own.

A blue sky awaits our final day in Lake Tahoe. Yesterday, we spent part of the day in Reno. Shopping a newly built shopping center, and later dinner at the El Dorado Casino. I played the blackjack tables at Circus Circus, and Silver Legacy. Losing early on, giving it almost all back, give or take two dollars.

The dinner was a third of what we'd paid in Las Vegas. All agree food, setting and price are much better at the El Dorado in Reno. A pleasant surprise, we eat salads, soups, meats, entrees and desserts.

Stuffed as we later watch a few shows at Circus Circus. One a group of Chinese girls catch tossed plates atop their head, high atop unicycles. Some taller than others. Later a limber Russian couple toss each other around the stage. Stealing a chair and then moments later sit on this chair atop the other's head.

We are entertained as is the crowd gathered. Some snap pictures, others applaud. The kids get another round of swimming. I watch others gamble. Still ahead days later, I may leave with my winnings instead of try for more.

It's a late start to morning. They sleep in. Perhaps mountain air, or their week of leisure catches up. Madeline thinks the buffets slow our pace.

They've taken breaks with card games and watching their weekly television programs. American Idol is one week closer to choosing the next idol in America. So too for the televised weigh in. Entertainment surrounds, sometimes a channel away.

We will drive to Sacramento tomorrow, then back to Portland the day afterwards. A long day of driving, yet many do this stretch in one day. Yesterday some were in mere long sleeve shirts, the sun keeping midday warm. Still there was wind and I was happy to have a sweater as an additional layer.

The sun keeps Tahoe bright. A nice change from often overcast Portland. Driving south we saw lamb, buffalo and advanced landscape. Sacramento is no doubt further along in their spring bloom.

We browsed an Apple computer store yesterday. They had the latest iPods, keyboards and computers on display. I read through a writing program on cassette disk. It helps outline and track our writing. I leave it on the shelf, thinking maybe it would limit writing.

The program would set us on a course, a preplanned course. One which may work yet takes some of the excitement out of writing - the art of writing. The sense of flow scrapped with each outline reminder.

Madeline calls wondering what is the day's plan. Specifically where we will have breakfast. It's back to Harrah's buffet atop their tower.

The one with banana French toast, fruit, salad, breakfast meats and eggs. Juice, coffee, croissants and desserts are also available. A buffet which slows our pace as the week progresses. Still we return for more. Views atop the casino tower are signature Lake Tahoe.

It's a majestic setting which takes us away for the day. Some return to experience it for a lifetime. Others leave with new memories. Travel opens up our lives. Not so much seeing new sights, rather leaving with a change in perspective which touches all aspects of life going forward.

There is now a cloud cover outside. The shadow of my writing hand distracts as does the Rap music blaring from hotel speakers. Not so much calm, rather Rap and other upbeat, high tempo music.

Music to help shrug off buffet lethargy and move us to gamble. Rick Astley now plays, "Together Forever." It helps get our morning writing done and adds to the experience overlooking blues of Lake Tahoe, greens of Sierra Nevada forest, and grays of the interspersed ledges.

Together, forever, we take this landscape with us after leaving a week of Nevada sun behind. Yesterday we walked to California for breakfast, crossing the street from Nevada lined casinos.

Today we will linger atop Harrah's. "Together forever with you," blares Casino music.

Today we leave for the central California sun. "Can I get the manager?" asks the front desk clerk Maira. Later the manager asks, "Is there anything I can do? Perhaps make the next trip more accommodating?" Realistically we won't stop in next time.

Lake Tahoe, a resort area in transition. Many locals speak of the good old days. A new crop of people show up for their own version of vacation. The scenery is signature Lake Tahoe, yet some accommodations are dated.

Time to upgrade the pool, hotel rooms and maybe even their websites. Some promise more than they deliver. "All those things are available upon request," they offer upon check out. A several star hotel should not expect guests to request in room coffee, a daily newspaper or even a refrigerator, let alone a sitting area with writing table. Still they ask if they can make our next trip more accommodating.

Not the resort experience we were expecting, or paid for. Today we drive down from the sixty two hundred foot level mountain lake to near sea level Sacramento. It's already mid sixty degrees in the California capital. We will shop the outlet mall before sitting poolside. We leave behind snow and dry mountain air.

Yesterday we took an hour side trip to Emerald Bay. I walked to the bank and asked if there was a nearby not to be missed tourist spot. The teller knew, mentioning often photographed Emerald Bay.

We drive along winding road, sections a climb with avalanche warnings. Drivers warned not to stop along this route. Later we find a pull out with walking paths, benches and breathtaking scenery.

Lake Tahoe at its best or so photographers would have us believe. It is a picture of contrast. Mid sixty degree weather with snowcapped mountains in the distance and nearby. Below us bay in various shades of blue, depending on the water's depth.

There are three Rav4's in the parking lot. Three of thirty vehicles the small Toyota sport utility vehicle. All three gray, one the newest model without a spare tire on its back door. We drive our own silver Rav4 back to the hotel for more swimming and blackjack.

The dealer continues his twenty or twenty one long enough for me to leave the table. A trip to Tahoe which didn't go as planned. Few vacations do and thus provide more to write about. We log it in, even when there is no writing desk available. Rotations, the detours along the way, fill our pages regardless where we sit to write them.

Chapter 8

———⟨⊰⊱⟩———

The sun is bright over Sacramento. The pool and hot tub are empty as we enjoy a leisurely breakfast. The kids manage one more spring break swim before we drive back to Portland later today.

Seventy degree clear skies is a surprise this last week of March. Tahoe hit mid sixty degrees with sidewalks and roadways covered in snow. The kids swim in the hotel pool with a girl also from Portland. Melissa visits with an older woman as she watches her granddaughter swim. She wants to swim longer now others are in the pool.

The Hotel Sierra is a surprise, with its beautiful lounge overlooking the pool area. This morning they offer ready to order omelets, French toast, pancakes and danishes. Starbucks coffee and juice are also available. I write this from the hotel room desk; the desk which is a living room away from the bed and sleep area.

An oversized hotel room we expected from the Lake Tahoe casino resort. Instead we spend four days overlooking a parking structure. This too creates a memory, although not the one we hoped or planned for.

I will finish writing my three pages then join them poolside. Yesterday the sun made for a perfect late afternoon sitting by the pool. I visited with parents of the kids' pool mate. They consider relocating to Sacramento.

Both had worked at Intel. Now the husband wants to relocate to the central California capital, twenty feet above sea level. His wife, Betsey, is reluctant to leave Portland, home for thirty five years.

Grandma is in no hurry to leave her retirement community either. Moving is stressful at any age. Exciting to think about the next locale, new friends, and better opportunities. Still at age eighty seven, moving is life changing, regardless how many decades we log in. Other times we wonder why we pursued the move in the first place.

The Sacramento area not immune to the ongoing recession, thus there are bargains in this housing market. Still selling the Portland home faces a similar economy. There are bargains to be found for buyers, regrettably it's not such a deal for sellers.

Lots to consider in relocating. Much more than merely the increase in sunshine and prospect of outdoor living for most of the year. The kids, schools, job prospects and how the nonworking spouse adjusts after leaving decade old friendship and networks must be considered.

Moving involves the entire family. Vacations too. We spend more time together and maybe in closer proximity, thus vacations are full of moments, some more memorable. We log in the daily which is never routine if on vacation. The more memorable ones at least, those which play music along the way.

Today it is a quick breakfast and then a full day driving from central California to Portland. A drive from the Sacramento area north through the Willamette Valley. Between there and here, Siskyoo Mountains, the high point along Interstate 5 - the west coast main north south route.

This morning it is already fifty degrees. Sacramento twenty degrees warmer than Portland, with blooming vegetation as proof. We extend our stay in Sacramento as sitting poolside in cloudless skies appeals, especially after record snowfall this past winter.

I sit poolside as kids yell to watch them dunk their heads. Later goggles help both of them swim under water. They learn how to do that on this vacation. Both swim, yet they weren't able to swim with their heads under water.

Their new found friend Jenna learns to swim on this trip to Sacramento. She lives on the other side of Portland. Her parents and grandmother spend a few days in Sacramento, part spring break, part house hunting. They like the California backyards, outdoor living for much of the year. Still they haven't found a place which says home.

Sacramento was the other area I considered relocating to twenty years ago. Portland won, although extra days of sunlight and longer summers would be nice, especially after months of Oregon rain.

We drive a bit of Sacramento in search of a place to eat. Many tree lined neighborhoods, homes tucked within small groves. Homes with lots of their own, not so much the crowded modern subdivision. Having neighbors on all sides perhaps protects our property when on vacation. The everyday living gets crowded, and leaves many wanting more yard, or a private backyard escape at a minimum.

Many of the homes our friends tour have a third living area, the outdoor patio room. Some with gazebo, or built in barbecue grill. Others with water features and terraced California gardens.

We reserved the hotels online. Lake Tahoe showed more than they deliver once we check in. Sacramento is a pleasant surprise and thus we extend for a day. That's always a good way to end spring break. Poolside to extend our memories of this family vacation to California sun, Nevada snow, and the casino buffets. There was even a Circus Circus act or three.

Chapter 9

Today it is back to routine; laundry, dental appointments and getting ready for school. Madeline is up early, eats breakfast and spends time reading. Abby lingers in bed until the last minute.

She leaves with a ponytail and backpack. She later returns for her water bottle and cold lunch. Suitcases are back in the garage. The car waits in the driveway as I'll run an errand later this morning before driving the kids to the dentist this afternoon. The dental office just called confirming my appointment tomorrow. A busy week for dental appointments as Melissa also has an appointment tomorrow morning.

A load of laundry whirls from across the house. Birds sing outside the window. Spring is slow in finding the Northwest. California weeks, if not a month ahead. They sit poolside as we rely on furnaces.

I have a list on my desk of things to accomplish. There are four birthdays coming up. Today an older sister turns fifty five. Usually we call on speaker phone to sing Happy Birthday. This morning didn't allow that as it's the first day back to school, after spring break.

I have a reminder to write first thing in the morning. Write daily, even while on vacation. Sometimes we have to remind ourselves, even on those days which write themselves. Those days we return home and restart daily routine. A backlog of mail and newspaper waits.

Flooding in North Dakota dominates the headlines. The viability of General Motors and Chrysler continue to make news. Today there is a plan to refund sales tax paid by those purchasing American made vehicles. This does little for residents in states without sales tax, Oregon included.

Oregon news centers on the retirement of state employees. Our PERS system once again is in peril. Dependent on market returns, the system appears doomed to fail, especially in this lingering recession. Tax payers will make up the difference. Over ten percent remain unemployed, thus even the income tax system suffers a reversal amid historic bailouts.

Interstate 5 is busy the entire ten hour drive north. Many on vacation, driving recreational vehicles - with car in tow. Others have several bicycles dangling from their rear bumper. Vacation, a time to leave town with family and sometimes our things along for the ride.

The gas stations benefit from increased traffic. Casinos are also busy. Surprising, considering how many fare after the past year and a half. Reno gives away hotel rooms. Tahoe advertises deals, yet sometimes comes up short delivering. Sacramento has two days of sunshine and offers a reasonable vacation for Oregonians.

My morning writing done, I'll drive to the bank before finishing birthday letters and more laundry. The kids are back in their school routine. No doubt a challenge for teachers this first day back from spring break. An adjustment from vacation to our everyday routines, even for adults.

Today is end of the first quarter. After months of decline, some hesitate to check their financial figures. Earlier in the month there was a rebound yet yesterday was more of the same, a major drop.

My sister called yesterday morning. She wants us to join them for a family wedding in July. I'd put this on the back burner due to the ongoing economic news. Still I check air fares and they are down. Many look forward to this summer's family celebration. We will wait a bit further before making definitive plans.

The economy keeps many close to home. Today I make another doctor's appointment. Something is wrong with my upper body. It may be a rotator cuff. Ideally physical therapy is all that is needed. Getting dressed is a chore; an exercise which stretches the limits of my arm's mobility.

This is not normal for me. Even the warm central California pool didn't entice me this time. My upper body aches, even while asleep. Tossing and turning painful enough to keep me awake.

We write of aches, pains amid our routine. Today there is no sun, rather another day of fifty degrees and drizzle. Maybe a more arid climate would help. Madeline has violin class. Abby has physical education, she reminds me slipping into her new sneakers. They both learned to swim under water while at the Sacramento hotel pool. They also came home with more school clothes.

The outlet mall was busy with shoppers. A nearby Applebees is boarded up and I wonder what happened to this newer establishment. We find a Spaghetti Factory restaurant outside Sacramento. This franchise opened its first restaurant in Portland in 1969. We go to the local one often. Eating out has tapered off yet is one treat we won't forgo altogether.

An airplane climbs, breaking an otherwise morning quiet. The coffee brews as this day gets a slow start. Melissa has an early morning dental appointment. I have an appointment for a cleaning at noon.

The kids got theirs cleaned late yesterday afternoon. A week of doctors appointments following spring break. The house is quiet as another airplane makes its way across the neighborhood. We write in the daily, our appointments and what goes on outside den windows.

My friend Marilyn drives in the school parking lot in front of us. She has her red Oldsmobile convertible this morning. Two school teachers are outside directing traffic, hurrying traffic along. The community asks school traffic move beyond the main thoroughfare.

Maybe a few more buses would address this issue. Few kids enjoy walking to school in rain. There are already enough sick children without more showing up drenched at seven forty five in the morning. It's another wet day as we close out the first quarter of a new year.

Chapter 10

Another day of rain for the Pacific Northwest. Forty degrees keeps it rain, unlike further north where snow falls, feet in places. Late in the season to continue with cold, rain or even snow.

Today I volunteer in Abby's class. The cortisone shot from yesterday keeps my upper arm in pain. Suppose it takes awhile before it breaks up stiffness in my shoulder. Yesterday, they gave me a shot and did blood work. Now I wait to hear from the physical therapy department.

They will get my rotator cuff operating again. It's been months since movement has been limited, even painful. It's now bothering my sleep and even getting dressed. My flexibility is challenged with each passing day. Let's hope it's only a rotator cuff and nothing more. Thus the blood test to check levels of calcium, potassium, and whatever else they find by examining blood.

We write in early morning. Some days pass and it is day's end when we log in our words. Today started out sore, and that's no April Fool's joke. Madeline offers to make toast as she sees me hobble along. "Do you want a second toast and coffee?" she later asks. I skip coffee until lunch, by then my arm feels better.

Early mornings aren't going well. I hope physical therapy clears up whatever limits my shoulder's mobility. Our body, something we take for granted until it slows down or grinds to a halt. Reaching is now painful.

We know limits and are familiar with our own physical limitations. Flexibility different for each of us, yet this has not been my normal for sometime, months even. Gradual and today there is something noticeably wrong. Even the kids help with breakfast before they head off to school.

Madeline has a shirt for a classmate who celebrates a birthday on April Fools day. Abby has library. Today she again wakes up the last minute possible and still manages to get in the car on time. We each have our own pace, some lollygag while others sleep in - then run.

Last night my niece from the San Francisco Bay area called. They will visit on Monday. It's their week for spring break. California has separate spring breaks by region. Not a bad idea for traffic, lodging and generating ongoing business.

We spent two days poolside in Sacramento. Seventy degrees and sun seems foreign in this colder Northwest drizzle. They have spring, even summer weather as our winter lingers, so too for our furnace which continues to heat the house.

Suppose like many springs we go from furnace to hot, with barely a week between the winter cold and summer air conditioning. We spend much of winter indoors. It will be nice to once again spend time outside. Not poolside, still it is refreshing to sit in the back patio once weather allows outdoor living. This is already the case for those in central California, not so much in northwest Oregon.

Chapter 11

This morning light rain falls. The dishwasher runs and I'm in the middle of my morning writing. Not so much middle, rather at the start. April begins as well.

A neighbor celebrates a birthday today, a day after April Fools. Yesterday I spent the morning logging in third grade students' reading speed. They have a second chance to read an article and hope their speed improves.

It does for them, although some have errors along the way. One hundred thousand catches a few off guard, thinking the number is ten thousand. People have trouble when too many zeros are added to their numbers.

Madeline has a book report due. She makes a chart of the narrative. A science fiction genre she decides. Abby has physical education. Soon they will play outside more, benefiting from exercise without realizing it.

Marilyn was in the school waiting area yesterday morning. We discuss spring break and our trip to Lake Tahoe. She is going to Lincoln City in a few weeks. She's also had trouble with her rotator cuff, both shoulders needed physical therapy.

She assures me they get better with exercise - time and exercise. I'm losing my patience waiting for things to get better. Shoulders never considered until they don't work as they once did.

We write of our day and those we meet along the way. Yesterday's vocabulary words were revenge, fiend and outsmart. The third grade students knew revenge. Outsmart they describe in detail. Fiend had us puzzled until we reread the paragraph which included fiend.

Reading lets us better understand another's point of view, if not learn new words. We in turn use better words further along. Crucifixion conjures up its own blood and gore. Suffering too. The other night we watched two hours of a movie portraying crucifixion.

It was graphic. Some wept as they watched Jesus and two others suffer. Sometimes a word, the right word describes the scene well enough. We don't need television or worse, the big screen. Words have meaning and thus we don't need a Hollywood produced visual.

Using the right word at the right time tells a story, gets the story across. Words alone move people. For many it is reading words rather than passively watching a video monitor which captures their imagination. Words placed in the proper sequence move as many.

Maybe the big screen attempts to outsmart readers among us. Still the revenge is reading rather than spend time viewing some else's choreography, blood and gore included.

An inhumane fiend read the third grade story. They had tied up a friend in a garden hose. A prank rather than a malicious scheme. Children are amused by the prank and later the kid who is tied up is busted for lying. He said it had been hours yet evidence in the hot backyard, the cool garden hose, tells another story.

Words get us in trouble so too for physical evidence which doesn't match our story. Had it been hours the summer sun would have made the garden hose much hotter. This too was in the third grade reading. Reading more than merely knowing word definitions; it's knowing what is behind them or in front of us, as it were.

I spent yesterday reading. I sat at the dining room table and placed my friend Chris's name on a note card next to the draft of my book, *A Sibling Within*. I began to read, doing my best to hear what my friend Chris would hear as he reads along. Chris in essence is the story's second reader.

Just then the telephone rings. It is the doctor's office. My blood sample from yesterday contains a high reading of potassium. Since this level could cause medical problems, could I come back in to verify. They take another blood sample and I return home to read my book further to Chris.

I wait by the telephone as I read. My friend's birthday is April sixth and I'll include a note, "Enjoy. You're in it!" along with my book. The one I e-mailed him about a year ago. It's now done, yet maybe he has insight on what to edit, add or delete. Perhaps he has a better idea for a front cover.

Ideally he enjoys reading along. I mention him three quarters through. That's also where the gist of the book is found. I write about how people leave, yet are often right beside us. They write and live by our side.

The furnace runs as it's barely thirty nine degrees this third day of April. Birds chirp outside as an airplane climbs in the distance. It should be seventy degrees by Sunday. I hope to get the lawn mowed during this first break in weather.

It's been a cold spring. I wonder if this has an affect on my joints. For months my shoulder has hurt. Thus the blood work to eliminate anything more serious than a rotator cuff. Abby slept to the last minute this morning. Madeline helps feed her breakfast and find shoes. Madeline excited about today's book report and the sleepover Saturday night.

I read more of my book while in the car waiting for them to cross the street from a day at school. Then after dinner I read the last twenty pages. The books on writing say to read our words out loud. Later read it through, thinking of someone in particular. Try to hear what they will as they read.

In the meantime, we send work on to them to find out what they really think of our book. True friends tell us. What we do with this information is up to each of us. In the end, we make changes for our self only, suggest books on the writing process.

Still it resonates with me. It is our writing, words, and voice. No one phrases it the way we do. It is our story to tell, regardless if we ruffle a few feathers along the way. This too is a good thing, otherwise our writing lacks spirit. It is blah, safe and boring. Writing demands we take a stand.

The furnace continues to warm the house this cold spring day as birds sing outside. My pen fills the page with words. Words which later are rewritten, edited and end by telling a story, often unknown in advance. We trust writing will reveal its words, and story.

We write of the everyday: the reading of books with a friend by our side, trips to the doctor's office for blood samples, or the wait by telephone. Invariably they call while we run errands or leave for dinner. As it works out, they call twice, even though I was home for the bulk of the day. Connecting with people is a challenge in writing books or waiting by the telephone. Leave and it will ring. Twice.

Chapter 12

Today we open blinds. Sunshine finds Portland. Although barely two degrees above freezing, the forecast calls for sunny sixty degrees by midday. There isn't a cloud, the blue sky interrupted by several jet contrails. The furnace turns back on even though I turned its thermostat down an hour ago.

Apparently the house loses heat quicker than early morning sun warms. Midday yesterday I turn on the television to see what is happening in our world. Binghamton, New York is in the news. Thirteen dead. This morning it is three police officers in Pittsburgh, gunned down answering a domestic violence call.

We are finally able to open the blinds here in Oregon. Still much of America prefers to keep their windows shuttered, or at least stay out of view. As a nation, we live amid violence.

Last night CNN debated autism. How, when and where this disease gets its start? Perhaps - why? Why is there a measurable increase in its occurrence? Even this is up for debate. Evidence reads different, depending on who reviews the data. Not unlike the cold garden hose which supposedly keeps the character bound for hours in our third grade reading.

Evidence doesn't lie, yet people draw varied conclusions based on their life experience or special training. We are all in the same boat, remember, or some would have us believe.

No further word from the medical lab, so my blood levels of potassium must be in the acceptable range. Late afternoon the physical therapist calls to set up an appointment.

They have details to fill in. They question whether I was in an accident or have an injury. Clearly I haven't been in an accident, still I'm not sure how to answer. I am injured, my shoulder no longer works properly. Without an "injury," I wouldn't be seeking medical help, specifically physical therapy.

We write of our day and news from across the country. We write of telephone calls we wait upon, and those which leave us puzzled. I'll see the physical therapist next Thursday for an assessment.

Sun warms the air and dries dew from the lawn. Later I may mow for the first time this spring. My niece, husband and four children will visit Monday. Ideally, I will be able to clean up the yard a bit. This has been a record snow year. Snow and ice damages much of the landscape. Still my shoulder will dictate how much yard work gets done.

Melissa will call Costco for another set of contact lenses. Madeline has a sleepover tonight. Abby and her watch "Daddy Daycare" on television. They have an assortment of children and activities planned yet few days go as planned for Eddie Murphy and his friends as they launch a daycare.

We write in early morning and the not so early morning. It's nearer eleven as pancakes cook, coffee brews and television delays the start of a new day. Today it is Pittsburgh. The sun shines in Portland, yet the whole country suffers at the loss of more innocent lives.

A woman interviewed says she watched in Binghamton in disbelief. From her window she had an across the street view, and only later does it occur to her to move away from the window. Some days go like this, other times we roll up blinds to allow the spring sunshine in.

Spring is here. People are in their yards planting, sweeping and enjoying a new day of sun. After a winter of record snow, people are energized to transform their yards. This means replanting several bushes if not trees lost during the snow and ice storm, a forty year record white December.

I cut back a few bushes, hydrangeas, and ground cover. Later I chip away at the moss covering our back patio. Today's sun will dry it out. I also move backyard furniture in place for the season. Perhaps this summer we will eat outside more often. It's usually too hot until late in the day, as the back patio and lawn are the south side of our home.

I move a few planters around and throw out yard debris, wood taken from the mimosa tree last fall. Then moss from between patio bricks and leftover bulbs from the hydrangea.

Birds chirp this morning. Earlier I went to Costco for paper towels, tuna and parmesan cheese. The place is packed, although midmorning Sunday. They have plants scattered about and many might spend this weekend setting up their flower pots and garden patches.

A car shifts in the distance. It is a quiet Sunday. We write in our day and plan for the week ahead. Madeline had a sleepover which reshuffles today's schedule. Last night we met a friend across town for dinner. The idea was to surprise our daughter Abby having our friend show up unexpectedly at the restaurant.

Instead I come in from cleaning the back patio and remind my wife of the time we are to meet at the restaurant. I later say our friend is interested in knowing how my yard work progresses. Thinking maybe Abby would buy our friend wants to know hour by hour how the yard work goes. Abby isn't fooled, her dinner surprise no longer a surprise.

We write of daily routine and the surprises throughout. We write a few pages a day and later, reread what we wrote and build on that. Sometimes there is a story within; a story within we aren't aware of at the start. We continue to write fresh pages, other times rereading our edited words. After awhile a story gets told. With each revisions, words become clearer, our story gels.

We write of the outside activity, people we meet along the way, even the backyard clean up gets logged in. Today it's late morning as I write my three pages. I've had breakfast, shopped Costco and reviewed some of the daily paper.

This week I'll start physical therapy for my shoulder. Surely they will leave me with homework, exercises to do on my own time. Down the road my shoulder will be back flexing as it should.

Dressing will no longer be a chore. Yard work will still be a nuisance, yet not the physical challenge a sore shoulder adds to the mix. Spring is here, a busy time of year, or at least we spend more time outside. Outdoors in sunshine in an otherwise often soggy Pacific Northwest.

The kids are off to school. Abby reminds me mom picks them up today. My niece visits and thus Melissa takes the afternoon off from work. She entertains and finds time to pick up the kids.

Madeline is packed for outdoor school midweek. She has her new sleeping bag rolled in its carrying case. The rest of her belongings go in a small separate bag. They are limited in what sixth grade students can pack. Still they come home with a laundry list for their three days of outdoor school later this week. They will study alongside the Pacific Ocean.

Birds sing as the dryer whirls a load of laundry. Today started off schedule and will no doubt continue off schedule. Off routine is better phrased, and this is another way of saying visitors are in town.

Earlier I asked the kids if they had clothes they outgrew. "Perhaps we should donate every other year," said Madeline. Abby has a few outfits she outgrew, doesn't like or "choke" - her word.

Still there is something about this pullover sweatshirt which doesn't fit, especially around the neck. I later find a few more shirts, sweaters and pants while rummaging through a pile in the garage. Garage, the pit stop before the final drop off at Goodwill.

Today is my brother's birthday. He is a year older and moves from the fifty year spot as does a good friend in New York. Birds are more plentiful this morning. I'd spent much of the weekend outside clearing some debris from the past winter. Sweeping the patio after scraping away moss.

Flower pots are now ready for new annuals, and will add color to the backyard. Today the dwarf white magnolia blooms. The street pear trees were in bloom three years ago while my brother and his wife were in town celebrating his birthday. They had a quick two day tour of the Portland area before seeing more family in Bellingham, Washington.

It's been weeks since hearing from the publishers. I had thirteen minor revisions and they said due to the backlog, it could take a month. Their literature says they print books in six weeks. Six months later, I wait for my first book to get published.

It's a long process writing hundreds of pages. It's proving to be a longer process moving a book through printing. I hope it moves more quickly off store shelves. At this point, I hope there are copies available for the late summer book signing at the beach.

Now the frogs chime in as an airplane climbs overhead. There will be relative quiet until my niece gets here with her four daughters, twin two year olds in the mix.

"Close your master bedroom door," says Abby. "Rita wandered in there last visit." Today, Abby is not youngest in the group. Still she tells us who will pick her up at school and which doors to close - or guard.

Chapter 13

———⟨⟩⟨⟩———

This morning I drop off a few letters at the school front office. Sixth grade students have mail call while at outdoor school along the Pacific Ocean. Madeline has her duffel packed and sleeping bag ready.

Today is the fourth of a series of summer days. I've cleared some of the debris left behind from this winter. Later I will mow the lawn for the first time this season. I will also drop tax returns in the mail box. Last night television news reported Californians now pay nearly eleven thousand to the state in taxes.

A dire situation, as more lose their jobs and no longer add to the state income. Still those numbers lead California toward the front of the tax burden line. A situation mirrored in many states, their budgets too are strained.

My niece and her husband visited yesterday. Their oldest is with grandma seeing the Grand Canyon. The other three are fast asleep when they drive in. It's been a long road trip north from California. We drove a similar route just two weeks earlier.

The dishwasher runs. The kids are dropped off early for student council. Abby returns to the car for her backpack. She slept in to the last minute and rushes through her morning routine. Later she stops as we enter the school, realizing she left her backpack in the car.

An airplane echoes in the distance. Yesterday someone stole one in Ontario, Canada and proceeds to fly just outside St Louis. F-16s follow him part of the way. He later wishes they'd shot him down. This Turkish man is in trouble with the authorities.

September eleventh changed many of the rules. Air travel perhaps the most impacted. Years later we address issues which can't be legislated, or maybe there is still someone ready to test those new rules.

"Portland gets better with each visit," says my niece. Suppose this depends where one starts, where Portland is compared to. Still Sacramento was a welcomed change from lingering gray overcast skies of this Portland spring. Landscape tells of the delay in spring weather.

Birds sing as I write in a few morning pages. Today it is back to routine. Tomorrow Abby has a state math test, thus I won't be volunteering in her classroom. I will send belated birthday cards. One to a friend in New York. Another to my brother a year older than me in upstate New York.

We write in early morning of our routine and visitors who break this routine. Sometimes some aren't along for the ride, rather telephoning their experience from the Grand Canyon. Thus this family takes two trips simultaneously.

Yesterday I retold a joke to my wife. Only in telling the punch line did I catch the joke itself. It was funny with books starting on chapter eleven, thus many pages were saved during this ongoing recession.

Still the punch line was that other chapter 11 - bankruptcy. Suppose we can joke about it, yet it's not a laughing matter. Sometimes we retell jokes to catch their punch line. Not unlike writing, which reminds us what we learn along the way.

My niece wanted a quick recap of Portland districts - its neighborhoods. It's hard to summarize sections of town, as most have changed during the past twenty years.

Geographically they remain in place, otherwise lots has changed within these neighborhoods, with new subdivisions which continue to grow along their periphery. The ones our company map quest for their sense of direction. I hope outdoor school for sixth grade students gives them more appreciation for nature, and the nature of things.

Chapter 14

The tree outside our dining room window still stands this morning. This past winter's snow and ice broke several branches. I trimmed it early on. Yesterday, I replanted. Many in Portland give their landscapes new plantings as well.

The street pear trees start to bloom. The cherry trees have been in bloom three weeks. Spring, a beautiful time of year in Portland.

My niece drives back today, they will notice vegetation fuller as they drive south. She says she enjoys those moments driving along open road with a van full of passengers fast asleep. It gives her time to think, in an otherwise hectic daily routine. Nature allows similar time away from the everyday, even though it is part of our everyday.

Writing, a routine activity which allows us to think past the immediate. To reflect on the not so routine in our day: our writing, guests, and blooming landscape outside the window. Sometimes we double check our transplanted trees still stand the next morning.

The dishwasher runs. Madeline's oversized Harry and David coffee mug is to my side. She left earlier with her duffel and sleeping bag for a few days at the coast. School outside the classroom for the remainder of this week.

Last night we discussed Holy Week. We previewed the individual days. Holy Thursday, the Last Supper. It's this and the washing of feet, service to fellow man. Holy Thursday much more than merely the Lord's last supper.

Good Friday, the Crucifixion. At three pm he dies on the cross. Friday the day to stop and reflect on the cross, the Crucifixion, the glory in suffering. Good Friday reminds there is meaning to suffering.

Four days of summer weather, today we are back to overcast skies and cooler temperatures. The birds remind spring is here, even if the sun refuses to stay along fulltime.

We reviewed Holy Week. We are reminded to participate in services as it is the only way to fully appreciate this defining week in the church year. My niece Erma comments she likes our kitchen tablecloth. It's a bunch of Easter eggs. She reminds me most of her mom at that age. The oldest and the two youngest, twins, are blue eyed blondes.

Maybe today I will hear from the book printers. They said it would take four weeks to make the edits. I sent them in promptly, having my first book printed is not something I'd call prompt. It's a long process as it works out.

We write daily with the hope a story unfolds within our words, within our everyday experience. We log it in trusting a story remains. We start with chirping birds and the overhead airplanes and go from there. Only later do we cut and paste, sort through our words as it were. They tell a better story this way. Stories started in the early morning, in early spring.

Today is a visit to the physical therapist. "Take an Advil," says my wife before leaving the house. I ask whether she's been to physical therapy. Perhaps they prefer to examine patient pain level without medication; Advil defeating a physical therapy consultation.

She leaves worried, still it is my medical appointment. Madeline spends a few days along the Pacific Ocean, science outside the classroom. She's been looking forward to this outdoor school for weeks. My wife worries for Madeline.

Worriers are entitled to worry. Trouble starts when they expect others to stop what they do and join them. They worry: for themselves, us, the shoulder pain, and outdoor school.

"The dinner chicken, be sure to cook it well," they warn. Meanwhile Abby sleeps in a few more minutes before hurrying through her morning routine. She doesn't have a care in the world, especially following a clock early morning.

Yesterday she had state wide math testing. She did well. We went to the Olive Garden to celebrate. Numbers come easily for her. We have our strengths. Success is a matter of building on strengths and surrounding ourselves with people who compliment our weaknesses.

The birds continue outside my window as coffee brews from the kitchen. While online I notice the print on demand publishing group has been bought by another publisher in Indiana. Consolidation continues, even in the developing field of self publishing.

The big publishing houses cut back. Major retailers have trouble moving books. Meanwhile the print on demand area grows - quickly. People write and bypass once solid gatekeepers at the big publishing houses.

"Every New Yorker is a writer," said a friend awhile back. The remark makes me laugh out loud, still everyone has a story. The trick is telling it in our own voice.

Worry is not part of my vocabulary, thus it would not ring true if I wrote endlessly on worry. It's a waste of time and doesn't help us move forward claim psychology books. Get busy with life, concentrate on what we can do, not so much lost in the problem or buried in worry.

We write of birds chirping, awakening our school aged children and the kitchen coffee. This morning there is no beep to signal it is ready. Maybe I didn't turn on the coffeepot. My morning writing almost done, I'll word a few more lines and then check that Abby is awake. Then I'll check on the coffee.

Maybe it got unplugged by accident. Later the physical therapist will do an evaluation as to why my shoulder has been sore for months. Ideally they have exercises readily available which will get my rotator cuff doing what it does naturally.

It's been awhile since my shoulder flexed as usual. It's been painful moving in some positions. "The coffee beeped ten minutes ago," says Abby. I must have been distracted by chirping birds, shoulder pain, and household worries.

Chapter 15

A neighbor drives away, her sport utility vehicle engine loud and cold. The four days of sun over, now it's wet and forty degrees. My niece times her visit well.

The standoff continues off the coast of Somalia. The boat captain is from Vermont. Underhill is a half hour from my parents home. His wife works with my cousin. Something happening off the coast of Africa hits close to home. I wondered why the Vermont governor contacted the family. Perhaps we don't think of Vermont and shipping - not in the same sentence at least.

Abby sleeps in. I'll wake her at the last minute as she prefers this routine. Madeline gets up on time and then takes it leisurely. I wonder how it is going at the beach. Did she sleep in or join the group for a sunrise walk?

Today I start the physical therapy routine. I was given exercises to do throughout the day. Ideally within weeks my rotator cuff is back doing what it does best. The therapist shows me how this part of the body, part of the shoulder operates. He has a doctorate, I wondered if maybe he had a degree in physiology, a masters perhaps.

He tells me the importance of posture. Not so much we look better without the slouch, rather bodies function better, our joints operate more easily. There is less chance of muscle and tissue rubbing against bone.

I leave with a few exercises and a pulley which slips over a door. It helps pull arms in positions they refuse to go. Or hurt lately on the way to flexing in those extended positions.

Body aches and pain make us appreciate our physical body all the more. It's nice going through the day without reminders of any particular muscle group, or joints which don't twist and bend like they once did.

There are four pages of medical history to fill in. They even take a picture of me. I wonder if this is to protect themselves. The paperwork insists it is to protect patients from medical fraud. Still I am taken aback as they take the photograph.

Within the same health provider yet records don't transfer. I fill in more information. Apparently we are not close to online medical records, seamless so they are readily available upon request.

This might be one of the few benefits of Hurricane Katrina. It makes us rethink how we do the everyday. Medical records get reconsidered. Logistics of all kinds get reviewed in an attempt to better respond to the next crisis.

Having mobility Is a good thing, even in the best of times. Imagine when crisis hits and we are immobile. Today we hear the Vermont sea captain made an attempt to escape his captors. Overpowering four thugs proves unsuccessful.

Meanwhile the United States Navy stands guard watching events unfold off the coast of Africa. A waterway full of pirates. Armed pirates yet another issue the new President faces.

Chapter 16

"Pirates," my daughter learns, "wear an eye patch so they can see during the day and allow them to focus at night." She just returned from several days of outdoor school. Science outside the classroom along the Pacific Ocean.

Madeline walked along the beach for a mile. She hiked through woods a couple more. She awoke early and saw the sunrise. So too for Mrs. Onstott. Perhaps it is the new routine or slippery rocks, either way she cuts her lip on a fall. Early morning, early on the sixth grade outdoor school adventure.

Yesterday I mailed contributions to our IRA's, a contribution for last year. We are a year behind in investments. We are late making contributions, our funds equally late in paying. Apparently it will be a much slower process of recovery. It was a quick slide taking some by surprise, others still perhaps unaware of the economic downturn.

For investors, it's been a dismal year. We look forward to the day our funds grow. Meanwhile thugs along the coast of Africa demand a two million dollar ransom. Let's hope the new administration can address this growing problem.

It would seem a world away yet shipping affects each of us. We are a world village, even this ship captain lives less than an hour from my childhood home.

I read through more of my draft to *Twice Found Postcards*. Later I tucked that story within the initially titled story of Las Vegas Farkles. Both center on places and people, places and people that become part of our permanent heart maps. We carry them onward, without requiring postcards to remind us.

Still some days it is this postcard falling from a book which reminds we have a story to write. We hold the pen as words flow. *Twice Found Postcards* recounts our trip to Las Vegas and a retirement month in Maui as my mother in law celebrates her freedom from the workplace.

We write of everyday and those places and people who join us along the way. Some linger longer than others. Madeline will keep her sixth grade class trip to the beach in her heart map. Heart maps, stories readily available ongoing.

We keep them for recycled laughs. They are stories we recount often and hold the most meaning. Maybe they change our life in some small way. A train whistles in the distance. It's another damp Sunday morning.

I was up late piecing together my third book. The publishers have not sent my first one back. I debate whether to send them an order for book two and three. They have reduced their prices fifty percent.

They state there is competition in self publishing as more people write. We write of everyday and the not so randomness of life. Like movies and music, now it is writers turn to do things independently. This means bypassing the big publishing house gatekeepers. Still story alone should market books, not so much an army of publicists.

I have orange juice to my side with a toast waiting to pop this Easter morning. Madeline altar serves, she carries a candle in the procession. Later we will drive to the beach.

A mild day, although filled with intermittent rain - rain, Easter bunnies and chocolate. I spent much of yesterday typing *Twice Found Postcards*. I edit as I type in the manuscript onto the computer. It's a review of a breakfast months ago. One with the kids as they are off school for a teacher in service day.

We hurry to the hotel and Madeline explains how watermelons are like writing. She is in sixth grade and learns further on the writing process. We learn ongoing, throughout life.

Abby prefers we not ask in advance what she plans to order, as we might change our particular order. It often does. We talk of writing and ordering restaurant meals. We linger while I jot down ideas for a book on my mother in law.

Later I fill in more of an outline which appears cobwebbed. It has branches going every which way. I've read these are more creative and thus less restrictive than the more numerical and alphabetical grid many consider outlines.

We write in spite of our scribbled outlines. Some stories start out titled, others already have an ending. Thus we start with a readily known destination. Other times we start in the middle and go from there. Books on writing often suggest start where we are.

That's Easter morning with orange juice to my side and Melissa yelling for the girls to get up. There are eggs and toast waiting, still they sleep in until the last minute. Actually, this morning they are awake and linger with their Easter baskets, bunny rabbits and stash of chocolate in the living room.

We will drive to the beach. Madeline just spent Wednesday through Friday there with her sixth grade outdoor school. She returns with stories; some on the accommodations, others on walks along the beach and within forest. She tells of her teacher slipping on a rock and cutting her lip. Early on Mrs. Onstott is injured. Then she mentions the science tidbits she's learned.

The length and weight of blue whales, their migratory patterns and the fact they don't eat humans. She learns of pirates and a bit about sea life. Oregon and science outside the classroom for this week's sixth grade lesson.

Madeline shares more lessons as we eat a late morning breakfast. She has just had another experience to fill part of her heart map. Those are always the best experiences, those we take along going forward, not unlike books which resonate, or reflect part of our own story.

Chapter 17

The kids are dropped off at school. They both slept in and later Abby sings through her morning routine. As adults we sometimes miss out on those moments which go by without a sense of time. For kids this might be an entire morning.

A morning routine unaware of time. They get their breakfast cereal and fluoride before heading out the door with backpack and water bottle in hand.

Yesterday we drove to the beach. Lincoln City was in a downpour. Still we manage an Easter brunch at Kyllos watching ocean spray a window away. Few tables have obstructed views at this oceanfront restaurant.

Later Melissa and the kids shop outlet stores. I wander through the casino. I leave with fifteen dollars from the blackjack table. Later I leave behind three of those at the gift shop. They have a wallet sized card on how to play hands of blackjack.

Still we may play by the rules yet come up short. Cards - a game of chance. A game often decided by how other table members play their hand. The luck of the dealer also plays into it. Casino games a clue as to why the economy continues to struggle. Even Einstein's best laid plans go amok as no two people invest the same way.

Many don't invest. Others take out their life savings at just the wrong time. They leave money on the table as it were. Still we may think we play the game with rule cards by our side, lots of it is luck; luck and how other members play their hand - their card.

Saturday I typed in more of *Twice Found Postcards*. The publishing houses say more people are writing. What matters at the end of the day are buyers. Are there readers for our books? We write hoping stories resonate with them.

While at the beach I read through a local newspaper. Someone had written science fiction of people living on other planets. The author says if he helps just one person further their goal, their plan, he feels rewarded. Specifically if he helps someone get through their book.

He wrote his and waits for Spielberg to call with a movie offer. I read thinking how many think our story is the story. The one others will read and maybe Hollywood will come calling. Still we write for ourselves, regardless what the writing manuals or even rule books tell us. We each write in our own voice and play our hand as it is dealt.

We may get angry if others don't play as we would, still it is their card to play, their story to phrase, their future to live. Early morning sun breaks through as planes climb in distant sky. We write with coffee by our side and a laundry list of things to do as a new week begins.

It's now time to log on the computer to review daily news and take care of business. Before then, I have a few exercises to get through, those recommended by the physical therapist last Thursday. Birds chirp outside as we log in more of our daily routine and exercise.

My morning exercises are done. My arms begin to flex as much as they once did. I'll see the physical therapist in two days. I hope they see my progress as well. I type in more of *Twice Found Postcards*. Today I will try typing the last thirty pages onto the computer. Then it's a series of edits before sending it for printing.

An airplane climbs in the distance. Writing is similar, we climb, logging in words on the page. Daily we add more.

Eventually we stop to reread what we've written, perhaps leveling in flight. Then we adjust ongoing, edit until satisfied with the result. Ideally a story remains once we remove bumps along the route, stray sentences which don't further the story.

Today it's barely mid thirty degrees. The calendar says mid April yet weather doesn't follow accordingly. Last night two rabbits ate in our backyard. They froze in place once the hail begins. I thought they would run for cover. Invariably when the kids leave school at three pm it rains or worse - hails.

The kids sleep in. Later they will have violin class and library. Abby wishes they had more time to make their book selection. Next year the elementary school will share some of its students with a newly built elementary school miles away. Maybe by then they will have more time to browse the library shelves. The outdoor recess playground will expand as well with less children.

The ship's captain is back safely in Vermont. Today we learn of three more hostages taken by pirates off the African coast. This yet another problem which must be addressed by the new administration.

Oregon unemployment now hovers at twelve percent. Nearly one in eight is unemployed. Not a good day for Oregon as it celebrates its one hundred fiftieth birthday.

Today my brother two years younger celebrates a birthday. It was also my grandmother's birthday. I tell the kids she would be near one hundred fifteen today. Still she would be nearer one hundred twenty five when we add up the years.

We write in the morning and later review pages of what we previously wrote. Sometimes there is a story found within. We might ask others for help. We ask their opinion on a book's front cover, title and those words beyond front cover and title.

People may offer suggestions, still it is our final decision. It's our story to tell, our writing reflected in the words. We are the ones whose name is on those words. We take responsibility for our writing exercise and those exercises prescribed by the physical therapist.

This morning I get the shoulder exercises done before sitting down to write. Tomorrow they will tell me how much my flexibility changed in one week. The results may surprise us both.

Later I will volunteer in Abby's class helping third grade students. The past few weeks I've tested their reading speed. They read one time through. Then hope their speed increases on the second reading. So far it has.

Like daily exercise, it builds our body's muscle and give us more flexibility. Maybe it gives us back some of our flexibility. Last night at Bible study they wondered who took Jesus from the cross? Did they themselves remove the nails? What were the burial procedures and time frames back then? Even today those first few days are harried experiences for those making funeral and burial arrangements. It's a time of grief yet there are many details to attend.

I finished inputting *Twice Found Postcards* on the computer. I read through more of it as I wait for the kids to cross the street and later as I wait for Bible study to begin.

Janice, who sits nearby, ask if my book is published. She is the second reader of my book. I tell her another book is being printed first. I want to tell her I finished another one since. The one on my mother in law and her postcard found within my reading material.

It tells of finding a book in Hawaii and again fifteen years later on our garage floor in Oregon. I'm only mid way through reading that book, still it is seed for a story. Later I would place *Twice Found Postcards* on a hotel bookshelf. I take *The Best of Families* and replace it with the book I just wrote on families - a family of lives including my mother in law with her postcard tucked within.

We write as traffic sounds in the distance. Our books are in various stages of being written, printed and read. We write ongoing just as life continues even if we wait for spring this year. Seasons change yet aren't always equally distributed.

Writing too progresses on its own schedule. We write before the prescribed physical therapy exercises, before breakfast and volunteering with third grade readers. We tell them we are working on it, getting our books printed. The publishing houses e-mail a similar response. We write of family - one sibling, one twice found postcard, one surprise sixtieth birthday at a time.

Chapter 18

Today I return to the physical therapist and find out if my flexibility improves. In the meantime my left shoulder is sore from exercise. I read through my latest series of morning pages. It recaps the everyday, places we see during Spring break and the progress of our books.

The publishing house called yesterday. I signed up for two more books while they have discounted rates. They will look further into why my first book is still in the printing process. Six weeks, leads to six months, now seven. Maybe we are all in the same boat. Or write how we will jump ship?

It takes awhile to get our words right on the page. Sometimes there are glitches in the printing process. They have recently expanded, then weather related problems. Last week they were purchased by a larger publishing company.

We write daily noting changes around us. Some we impact by our own exercise, others happening on their own, in spite of us. Madeline wants to practice violin with her friends. Later she returns excited to tell me she has them coming over tomorrow for a slumber party. Thus they will practice and chat as sixth grade girls do.

Abby needs more lunch money in her school account. Yesterday we read of pigs which had their own running track. Another book has us cooking vegetable stew. The third group read of making a swimming pool; start with a stream and add logs.

We read every Wednesday in the school atrium. Marilyn is there too. She wonders if my book will be ready before the end of the school year. I tell her I've just finished typing in another, *Twice Found Postcards*. She looks at me strange.

She too has those moments I describe yet they pass by her. Writers log them in. We write of postcards which fall from our books. The lobby full of Tenderloin district residents who have stories of their own.

The story of where they now live or how they manage to land in subsidized housing. Many had fuller daily schedules before life sends them a curve. Most stories start in this curve, the rotations in life.

We write ongoing and eventually a story remains. Often a story with a few curves, blended within. Some we place, others write themselves in. We write longhand, then edit while typing our words onto the computer.

They are more legible at this point and we hope sound more like a story. From there it's a matter of editing; editing and listening for those twists in plot, which tie the story together.

The curves write our story. The sore left shoulder, the delay in getting our books printed, and those who sit besides us and help edit. Others ask if we write, what we read, or even what we write about. Some days we are the last to find out. Other times we are a story's first reader as we look within our morning pages in search of story, or seeds to story.

Yesterday was one of those days, full of story seed. Dead ends, road closed signs amid story seeds. I drive to the physical therapist bypassing the interstate. Instead, I drive through city streets I rarely pass through.

Some don't. Instead they abruptly end, turn to gravel or greet with a "Road Closed" sign. I turn around onto another street which dead ends.

"Last Street," reads this sign. It too dead ends. This kind of day, still I drive further to the physical therapist. He asks how my week and day are going. Later I hand pedal for five minutes. I am told to change direction at one minute intervals. My right arm barely noticing as I pedal. My left shoulder thawing, is the term for this ache, burning sensation.

Then he shows me how to lean into a door frame. I know this one will hurt, and probably heal whatever is wrong in the rotator cuff. Later, I am given a latex strap to hang atop a door and stretch away. Three different positions, some more painful than others.

The exercises over I drive to lunch with my wife. Lots of construction around her office building makes it difficult to find a Wells Fargo branch. The first stop is their home mortgage processing branch. The second a mere automatic teller machine.

Somewhere there must by a Wells Fargo which will take my payment in person. I later find this person behind a bullet proof glass, the one with long line and pleasant teller. She too asks, " How's your day going?" Oh, it's going!

Later I read through my fourth book I hope to someday publish. Untitled, I wasn't sure where those one hundred fifteen pages would lead. I complete a first edit on my morning pages, rereading what I wrote for the past month or more. The daily routine, travels, our ongoing life, including the days which run smooth and those we try getting through, in spite the road blocks and dead ends.

I sit in the car waiting for the kids to get out of school. At home the publishers have the second copy of my book on finding meaningful work ready for its second edit. Meanwhile my oldest brother calls. This is probably the fifth time he ever calls. It's rarely good news.

Instead he wonders what I know about Fairpoint Communications. Their stock is down seventy percent and wonders if it might be a bargain. The short answer - who knows?

Today all bets are off. What was certain just years ago, isn't necessarily so today. He also offers we can stay with them while in town for a July wedding. We haven't decided yet on going back east.

I print from our home office Canon printer my first book I've ever sent to publishers. I read through half of it. A Gallup pollster called earlier. They question across the board. I may consider my present life on figurative rung eight, still like many Americans I'm not happy with current state of affairs.

As a matter of fact I saw a dentist within the last year, a medical doctor within the last month. "No" - to daily fruit and vegetables. I write about incoming telephone calls and their survey questions. I mention my books just in case the surveyor finds free time.

I suggest most everyone writes today. Each of our books as valid as the next person's story. He studies forensic science. There is a story there out of Lincoln, Nebraska. Nebraska home to Mr. Gallup who keeps things surveyed.

I was mid letter to my brother who celebrated a birthday earlier this month. I am in the process of writing another brother who's birthday was days ago, and a sister who's birthday I missed the end of last month.

My brother in Philadelphia calls. Our oldest sister is in town visiting our parents. It's a surprise visit as she gets groceries and drives through town to their home. On the way she picks up my father who walks the village blocks. His car is at the shop and he gets in exercise at age eighty eight while waiting for the car repair.

We write of birds chirping outside, slumber parties in the family room and those incoming telephone calls. Lately there have been a lot of unusual telephone calls and correspondence.

My oldest brother who doesn't use technology calls.

The Gallup poll people call.

The book publishers send a second e-proof of my book.

"There must be an abundance of mercury circulating," I tell my wife. Mercury, the god of communication.

Chapter 19

Yesterday, I read the second half of my first book printed. No book is ever complete. There are run on sentences and a few sentence fragments. Still I find only two typographical errors and hope readers don't find more. I'm part Irish and thus it's ok to include a few intentional errors in our work.

Last night I read a third of the way through *A Sibling Within*. Today I plan to read through the rest. By Monday I hope to have the editing done and send that book to the print on demand publisher.

Then I'll work on Redealt Postcards. This one has been difficult to title. This morning I think I will go with *Twice Found Postcards*. It's a story of finding a postcard within a book from someone long gone. They passed away over six years ago. Las Vegas is also tucked in there, the Las Vegas which farkles long after we leave this desert winner wonderland.

My oldest brother mentions a cousin recently visited Las Vegas. He says a lot of construction projects are stopped mid job. Another cousin works with the wife of the ship captain who was held by pirates. They both work in the same Vermont hospital emergency room.

We find postcards within our books from people who have long since passed. We watch horror stories off the coast of Africa yet some of those characters live miles away from our childhood homes.

We write of everyday and those people and events that aren't. We fill in pages one word, one telephone call, one birthday at a time.

Today Abby goes to a classmates birthday party. Last night she laments she is down to one friend. Abby is having a bad week.

Two nights ago, she was in tears about her homework. I hope I put an end to her working against deadlines. It too leaves us distraught, it reshuffles our routine. Then again sometimes we run late in our own homework, sending off delayed birthday greetings as it were.

It's a sunny spring morning. By midday it will feel like summer. Shorts weather and it's been awhile since the sun has covered our area. Madeline just stopped in wondering if I want a biscuit with egg and bacon; a sandwich or separate. "It doesn't matter," I tell her.

She leaves to further breakfast. The birds continue outside my window. Yesterday there was a sixtieth birthday invitation. My oldest brother turns a new decade early May. I'm ten years younger than him. My youngest sister, eleven years younger, thus I'm a middle child.

We write of breakfast orders, singing birds or even family birth order. They all matter, some more than others. I read through more of *A Sibling Within*. I add an older sister experiences Hurricane Katrina first hand. Most family find out mid storm our sister is in town visiting New Orleans. This too is story seed.

We write of the everyday and those vacations which don't go as planned. Today the children liturgy centers on faith and community. First we doubt on our way to faith. Faith in action leads to community. We live better in community.

Still our individual communities vary. I wrote on their disparity. *A Sibling Within* recounts a front lobby of story within San Francisco's Tenderloin district. I also mention my sibling within, noting how those who left long ago, are often still beside us as we write, live and place breakfast orders.

We write daily and later edit to add or, take from there. Still later we check for grammar, punctuation and conversational tone. We place the reader beside us, we include them and ourselves in stories. Writing a conversation we place ourselves within.

I finished editing my second book, I'll send off to publishers. Now I have to input the revisions. Then read once again, thinking how someone specific will hear our words. Editing forces us to listen to what future readers might hear. Today, it's my college roommate I envision listening as I edit this story.

Sooner or later a story remains. One which has heat, soul and message. One which resonates with us and we hope future readers. We write of the surprise birthday parties, the sunshine amid our everyday routine. Some days are more routine than others. Some start off late, others greet us with birds chirping in summer sunlight. An airplane flies over this early morning.

Airfares have been lower recently. I may check on flights and surprise my older brother along with the rest of the party goers. Sixty as good as any age to celebrate. My oldest brother called three days ago. Does he know something is in the works? He doesn't call often. Age sixty calls nonetheless.

Birds sing outside with increasing regularity and volume. They are back! Spring must be here. Still the calendar says it is May in a week. From furnace to air conditioner again this weather cycle.

We write daily using our words as we run errands, or make future plans. We write of the things seen along the route and those we sit down to listen in on. Yesterday I walked four miles, at the end were two blisters and a religious music concert. The Everett songwriter sang for an hour.

Then we drove home as my wife and kids met me at the church concert. We write of the birds, music concerts and those bumper stickers or license plates which make us pause.

Today I'll e-mail the publishers. I finished reading through the second e-proof of my book on finding meaningful work. I'll e-mail they can send along the actual book in book form for one last read through. Then the book which was finished last September will be available for readers.

A radio report says Kelly Clarkson always buys her album the first day it is available. She goes to iTunes first and buys a second at a brick and mortar music store. Maybe I'll order online and visit a bookstore as well. I understand how Kelly feels buying our own work, words, or music.

We hope others enjoy our work, and effort. Still like all art it is in the doing. Success is on our own terms. In other words, the success which matters is our own personal success. Still having the world feel the same is welcomed.

My friend who also volunteers for Wednesday third grade reading says she loved *A Sibling Within*. She tears up as she tells me parts which resonate, hit home with her. This too makes for a memorable day.

We write in early morning while birds sing outside and kids sleep in. We write before the day begins in earnest. There are daily exercises to get through. Breakfast, bills and now a green lawn needs mowing. We add this to our routine as well.

Later this summer we will spend time watering this lawn and yard of plants, shrubs and flowers which survive without a green thumb. Some keep a house full of live plants. I thought the roof overhang at our first home did them in.

Now a three story house blocks our east side windows. We were here first and now the plants aren't here anymore. Few plants grow indoors, although birds sing and grass grows outside. Our writing captures some of this sound, growth, and movement.

Yesterday, I e-mailed I was satisfied with the second e-proof of my book on listening to life and taking it from there. "Send me a printed copy of the book," I e-mailed the publisher. This is a process started back in September, it's now approaching May.

Maybe it's on its own perfect schedule as there are even more people unemployed, jobless and not merely this year's class of graduates. We write on the everyday. The rush to get kids to school, birds outside and the spring blooms. Today they have student council and are up earlier; earlier looking for socks and matching clothes.

I read through half of *A Sibling Within*. Writing becomes complicated when we stop to think of the various time frames involved. Still I went ahead and put more of the narrative in present tense, although much of the story happened long ago. Lived once long ago, now becoming fiction as I write further along.

A good friend is in the hospital. Something in his legs among other aches and pains. I've four sessions left with the physical therapist. My shoulder hurts. Can only imagine what it feels like when our entire body aches, and swelling legs prevent us from moving. Thus our friend lies in a hospital bed again today.

Last night a market researcher called from Philadelphia. I cut the call short as I was expecting a hospital report. Midday our ninety six year old friend calls our cell phone. I rarely get calls on this line and am surprised to hear her voice. She is checking up on us, her daughter's whereabouts and how her son in law is doing.

She turns ninety seven in August. We should all be making telephone calls at that age. I first thought she may be stranded somewhere. She too once kept an active lifestyle. Not so much today as she stays close to her apartment and the community room.

I'll place one of my books on her community room bookshelf. She is mentioned in my book. It is a thrill to include her. I hope she and other residents enjoy reading her insight on life and longevity. She knows.

Melissa came home with good news. It is good news a co-worker finds work at the Washington branch office. No more commute into Oregon, no more Oregon state tax.

Still this is someone my wife worked with for eleven years so isn't such good news for my wife. We just celebrated her birthday together a few weeks ago. Our elderly friend passed through Philadelphia en-route to Portland.

My wife's co-worker Denise started life in Philadelphia. Just now a neighbor starts their lawn mower. I got through the second round of lawn mowing for the season yesterday. Lawns come back to life as birds sing on the sidelines. Today I will bring the second part of *A Sibling Within* into the present. We write ongoing, giving our writing voice. It sounds better and reads easier as it captures story within the present tense.

Today I volunteer in Abby's class. They will read further in their chapter books. Last week we read of pig marathons, cooking stews and building swimming pools.

They get better at reading as the year progresses. I hope the physical therapy people say something similar tomorrow. Week two of stretches and exercises; getting shoulders to do what they normally do naturally.

Two days of summer heat are now replaced with cloudy sixty degree weather. I will visit with a friend who spends a few days in the hospital, I hope they get him mobile once again.

I spent much of yesterday editing *A Sibling Within*. I will read through again the tenth time according to my notes. Yesterday I read thinking how Clare would hear my words. We spent three years of college together. She too is an Accounting major, although a year ahead. We've lost touch through the years, yet she is a computer search away.

I may send her a copy of my book. Seeing our books on bookstore shelves is exciting. Sending friends our words ordered from online bookstores is as exciting to ponder. How will they react? We hope they enjoy what we've written and also getting back in touch. College now almost twenty five years later.

This year I turn fifty, like the famous sign which greets visitors to Las Vegas. It's survived those years with tourist snapping pictures of the flashing sign along Las Vegas Boulevard. I walked by it last summer on my walk from our hotel to The Strip. The sun set while airplanes land nearby; close by as they land minutes later at McCarren field.

We write of day to day, birds outside and of our walks in desert sun summers ago. The kids sleep in. Melissa too. Last night she was held up in traffic over two hours. This adds to the everyday commute. Later she is grateful to find a nearby gas station.

For some this might be their daily routine - traffic. My oldest brother wonders why the high housing prices in Portland. "The ocean is over an hour away?" he questions. I want to tell him it's quality of life. Surely he will figure it out as do those who continue to relocate to the Rose City.

Game two of the NBA playoffs. Portland is back in the game. Maybe this added to last night's traffic. "Grease" also performed downtown and perhaps adds even more traffic. Portland prices are high due to quality of life, weather and being wedged between two much more expensive real estate markets. This keeps Portland afloat, although some surveys like to paint us unhappy. Now it's time for the kids to begin their daily routine, which starts with waking up.

Today is the annual, "Bring your kids to work" day. They see behind the scenes to their parents everyday, their work day. The place and people they spend most time with on a daily basis - their nine to five family.

I have physical therapy midday. I thought I might take a trip to the beach and my wife is quick to remind me I have a doctor's appointment; midday it will keep me close to home. Not so much the shoulder as it is noticed less with each passing day.

Instead my whole body aches from the increase in exercise. I spent part of yesterday morning reading further along with third grade students living a la boxcar and on inheritances gone bad. "Why aren't any of the boys heirs?" one third grade student asks. I explain the word heir to them, pronunciation and its implication to those who inherit.

Later I visited with a friend in the hospital. His mobility is limited and later the family leaves in search of a care facility. My friend will spend over a week with his own personal physical therapist. One I hope gets him back up and walking. Still his driving days are over. Never a good day when car keys are taken away, and that's going on year three for him.

Going back to the hospital parking lot, I meet someone struggling with the elevator. It's one of those where we go up a floor to get the bridge leading to the hospital. It reminds me of our recent trip to Lake Tahoe. The person struggling has a Las Vegas sweatshirt on.

Originally from Greece, the heat of Las Vegas doesn't bother him. I ask if the Dallas heat is worse than Las Vegas. He reminds me he is from Greece and most places seem cool in comparison, even Dallas his present home.

Marilyn waits in the school atrium. Only later does the teacher let her know they have a special event and don't require her assistance. She is not amused. Still we visit before I read alongside third grade students. This morning we read along with their history wall of Portland bridges.

One reads, "That ends our project." Another reads one bridge "required maintenance after a hole was found in 1971." Earlier this student mentions the bridge was built in 1973. While it may be hard for third grade students to keep accurate timelines, Portland does have a dozen bridges. Some famous setting records when constructed, while others hold records even today.

We write of everyday, laundry whirling, the kids accompanying their parents to work, and our hospital visits. We write of routine and books which take us out of routine. I found one yesterday on the art of listening. It's on listening to music specifically, still it hones each of our listening skills, music or otherwise.

Writing is listening for story. We find words, listening in on the everyday. Pens click, airplanes fly in the distance, the everyday is reflected within our writing. We log it in, only later going back to check agreements.

Keep it present tense and conversational. We want readers beside us as we help them maneuver parking garage elevators. They hear third grade students read of wet potatoes instead of wet newspapers. We listen for story as we write further.

"Don't leave without your story," said my daughter Madeline awhile back. Her words echo as I leave for physical therapy with my manuscript. I'll read a bit further in the car before the midday appointment.

Later I read further as I enjoy chicken fajitas and a margarita. The pages go back inside my manila envelope, as I linger in the Mexican restaurant. I stop into a nearby Goodwill store to browse their bookshelves. The lady originally from Romania is behind the checkout counter. By the time I leave with a book on writing scripts and one on retirement secrets, she is replaced with two Asian women.

I read a bit of both books once home. The retirement one has a note from someone's mom and dad. "Don't do what we've done or else you'll need this book," it reads. This book covers finance, fitness and our future.

The other book is on selling scripts. All stories require a beginning, middle and end the book reminds us. Still having an agent or someone who knows people opens doors and forwards scripts. Not so much words, rather marketing moves scripts, whether for feature films, television sitcoms or alternative media.

We write of books on our desk, and those en route. Yesterday the publishers e-mailed my book on listening to life has been shipped. An e-mail also comes in from United Parcel Service. My first book is en-route, expect it in six to nine days. The UPS e-mail says to expect it Monday. It's been expected since September, eight months ago.

Many talk about writing a book for much of life. Someday this becomes a reality. Now we just wait for the delivery. Today I will leave with my story, the second book *A Sibling Within*. It's already written, now a matter of taking away a few words, or adding more.

We read our words in the edit process. First slow, aloud, we reread and as often rewrite what we once wrote. It's the same story only now we hope told in a more concise, if not flowing manner. Writing which keeps our interest and interest of the reading public.

The book on selling scripts reminds good writing alone can't salvage a story. The story has to be there. As television and movies mature, it is arguably more difficult to come up with new stories, a new storyline.

Still those which get past gatekeepers are the original ones. The ones written from those unique and special circumstances - ones written from the person in that particular situation which allows them to write such moving words. Their situation moves them and they in turn move us.

Later studios rework the script, rewrite the words. Ironically the writer often has little say in the final edit. Their story now told by others, not only to others. Writing speaks, regardless who tells the story, still translating another's experience is perilous.

Keep an agent, lawyer ready. It helps to know people who know people. This too can bring scripts forward. Marketing alive and well in America. Words on the other hand sometimes struggle.

Yesterday, I made a reservation for a flight to Philadelphia. From there I will drive with my brother to Vermont where our oldest brother celebrates his surprise sixtieth birthday. Not so much surprised he turns sixty, rather many will be in town to see him turn a new decade. He is first to do things in our family.

Sort of. He is the oldest yet is not fond of water nor flight. We are limited by fears. My daughter stays away from dogs, even small barking ones. Phobias are irrational at best.

We write of travel plans, fears, and our everyday. Yesterday I read through a third of *A Sibling Within*. I'll input revisions and mail it off soon. My goal is to send that book to the printers before this trip back east.

Meanwhile my first book should be here early in the week. I'll quickly read through and then e-mail they can now begin selling this book. It's a quick read, having read through it perhaps twenty times, if not more. This and the fact we wrote those words. Thus we read at a fast pace and ideally the words which resonate with us, resonate with others.

Today is barely forty degrees. By midday it will warm, still spring has difficulty maintaining warm weather. Abby went to the symphony yesterday. "One kid slept through part of it," she said. She sat beside another class. There are perils to being front of the line. Abigail is often first should they place them alphabetical by first name.

While writing my brother in Philadelphia with the flight itinerary, a pollster calls from Allentown, Pennsylvania. She wants to know how we feel about the economy, our spending habits and outlook for the future.

How do we plan to manage long term health care? Do we pay for radio service? Do we own a big screen television, subscribe to cable a la maximum? Those kind of questions and whether we are republican, democrat or independent?

Suppose by the time she gets to this particular question, even telephone surveyors know our party affiliation. Clearly we answer some of those questions depending on how we see ourselves. How we see ourselves within the economy, our role within the economy?

Do we contribute or expect others to pick up the pieces? Do we expect great things from government or do we rely on ourselves to face the future on our own terms? The survey reinforces how much of America's everyday is in consumption.

While not actively shopping, we are offered buying ideas from the television screen. She asks whether we review television programs and movies from online? In essence people live between television and their computer. A virtual world for too many.

Perhaps this is why there are now surveys on America's health care. What do they do right? What they do wrong? How we fit in? We take surveys as we each reflect on our own lives, our personal economic realities.

Clearly many readjust their screens as they go forward. The past year's show has been a downer. The show goes on nonetheless.

Even sixtieth birthday parties break routine and are celebrated. Ideally there are a few surprises left for the birthday boy.

My goal was to get edit revisions on the computer before I leave on vacation. Yesterday I did half then we went out for lunch, an early Mothers Day celebration. Today we will go for brunch, another Mothers Day celebration - early.

I finish inputting my revisions on the computer. Mid afternoon through early evening I type. Later I read aloud the first few pages and then the final page. "Wow. Your writing improves," says my wife. The last page has her in tears. Tears during the final edit is always a good thing. "Tears in the writer, tears in the reader," said Robert Frost.

People get engrossed in their reading material. Writing travels, only later do readers travel alongside us and our words. Ideally they travel alongside blending our words, our story to add adventure to theirs.

Writing allow us to leave home without stepping out the front door. Reading allows much the same. Sometimes writers share their journey with us - whether in having books published, moving through everyday routines, or the breaks stopping for Mothers Day celebrations. Early celebrations and late birthday parties. Birthday parties which surprise even sixty year olds.

We write daily and months later reread what we wrote. Often within our words are threads to a story. Only then do we rework and reword them. Editing tells the same story, only better. We write, edit and hope one day our story is told. We no longer can improve on our words.

Now it is up to the reader to take our words and improve on them. Each of us reads a story different depending on what is going on in our lives. What happened before and maybe even what we plan for ourselves in the future.

We write in the early morning. This is often the calm in our day as we hear birds outside our window, the click of our writing instrument, and the idleness of a new day. We write to capture those moments of quiet within an otherwise busy world.

Later we will join traffic, noise, the busyness of routine. An airplane climbs as the kids sleep a few more minutes. We have plans today. We have reservations for a Mothers Day celebration.

Early reservations as that day is still weeks away. Still it coincides with my brother's sixtieth and I won't be in town. Then again, I'll be in town for my own mother's Mothers Day. No cake for her say doctors, yet special occasions call for one.

It's barely forty degrees again this morning. The birds sing outside as plants bloom. Still it does not feel like May is days away. Calendars say otherwise.

Brunch is a pleasant surprise. The place is not full although food is back up to par. We eat and watch Columbia River traffic a window away. The Interstate 5 bridge lifts to allow a ship through on occasion.

Later we walk the Red Lion Hotel at Jantzen Beach. I show the kids where I sat and wrote *Twice Found Postcards*. They see the fourth floor lobby area, view of river and Interstate 5 bridge outside a wall of windows. The comfortable couches and chairs are removed as they either clean or upgrade the hotel furniture. The hallway bookcase is also missing.

Still bookcases in the hall at the other end of the hotel contain books ready to be swapped among hotel guests. "This is one spot I'll use to circulate my book," I tell my wife and kids. Hotels for people going places, thus I hope they take my book along with them. One day the right person finds just the right book at the right time. My book gets read by someone who takes it further. Ideally this happens often.

The best books never return to the bookshelf. We read and later apply the book's message or theme. If what we read resonates we in turn live different then and each day going forward.

After brunch the kids play school. They have notes and stuffed animals in the mix. I read a third of the way through a draft of *Twice Found Postcards*. It recounts a breakfast we had once they were off school due to a teacher in service day. Madeline relays stories are like watermelons, or so insists her sixth grade teacher. Abby is in the story too, her everyday, menu selections and reading in her third grade classroom.

They listen as I read about their grandmother. The one with a smoking Mercedes, crescent moon postcard and retirement party in Maui. We write of people, places, and moments. Some more cherished than others.

Madeline reads a book for a book report due tomorrow. "Keep reading," she says. "I can listen to both books."

I let her continue with hers. I'll edit mine later on my own. They already know parts of the story as they are weaved within. We write of everyday and the people who share our everyday. We write of current events and of times long ago. Those moments captured on postcards or even books we once read.

Sometimes where we find books holds a story, or even where we sit to write one of our own. We stopped into this hotel writing nook, so later the kids can tell me whether I'm successful in bringing them back with my words. Words transport us. They take us from cold spring mornings, to hot brunches, and the writing nooks in between.

Chapter 20

Today I wait for a special book. The publishers e-mailed last Thursday saying my first book is being shipped. Later UPS sends an e-mail so I can track the delivery.

Yesterday the UPS tracking listed my book being received in Portland. Earlier it had stopped in Redmond, Washington on its way from Vancouver Island. It takes awhile to write a book. We spend a lot of time rewriting, editing.

Writing is rewriting for the most part. Then we wait for the printing process. We double check e-proofs then read through our words now bound in book form. This is the copy I wait for today in cold Oregon rain.

May is less than a week away with little sign of spring, much less summer. I'll read through words I wrote last fall and some long before. Then I'll send the publisher a final approval so they can release my book.

I read releasing books is akin to sending children into the world. Will they be ok? Will they be accepted? Will they succeed? So too for our words, long in coming, figuratively and literally as I wait for the brown UPS truck to deliver a book which records part of my life and ideally entertains future readers.

Books affect each of us differently even though reading the same words, the same story. It's taken months longer than expected to produce this book. A bookstore salesperson notes writing books is "a learning adventure." She also alludes to the selling of books.

Most authors hope their words travel quickly. Initially word of mouth and then the book takes off. It's no longer coming in on a slow UPS delivery, rather going out, distributed as quickly as possible. People want to spent time with our words, story - us. It's our hope they see themselves reflected within those words. In essence, it is part their story too.

We write with the hope it relates to them. We write in early Oregon rain, while a neighbor's high school son warms his vehicle before driving to a final few weeks of school. We write of the daily and not so daily events of everyday. Today I wait for my first book published.

The ongoing delays add excitement, anticipation. This an example of doing something for the first time. Regardless how many books we may write, moving the first one through the system holds our memory. This one starts the process.

I've read through drafts of *A Sibling Within* several times. Still there is more editing to do. Once I read through it again it too will be ready for the printing process. Birds sing outside, as the shadow of my writing hand moves along the page. I have exercises to finish. Twice daily they help my rotator cuff move again encourage the physical therapists.

"You kill me," says Abby as I remind her to take her fluoride and vitamins. I'd like to think I have her best interest at heart in days of swine flu, global swine flu. Madeline leaves with her violin. She has a concert this weekend and another slumber party.

She enjoys sixth grade. This was also one of my more enjoyable grades. My teacher, was a nun, Sr. Doris. Days after that school year ended, I lost a younger sibling, my own sister Doris. We write of everyday and those days which stop us in our tracks or even while we track down UPS deliveries.

The UPS truck finally gets here. I stay home in case I have to sign for the package. The driver hands me the book. He notes the kids must have just received a new camera as they take his picture: him, his truck, and my first book from the publishers.

I tell the driver it is much better than a camera, it's my long awaited book.

I spare him details I thought this would be a six week process, not the seven month ordeal. Still it's a fun day when we have our words in hand. We have the cover the way we once envisioned.

There are a few papers inserted along with the book. A final form to return before they release it and print copies for future readers. There is another form for the final revisions. I read through and decide it is ready, or at least good enough for my first effort at writing.

There is also a price sheet. We need to cover printing and marketing costs. Thus the minimum is stated as twelve dollars. In college Marketing class they said to place a 99 cents in the figure. In other words people perceive 19.99 as much less than twenty dollars.

I wonder if I shouldn't go with a clever 12.34 or maybe the doubling of digits as in 12.48. Still, I go with 12.25, and hope it makes a few purchasers smile. The idea is having them smile as they turn the last few pages.

My first book is about finding meaningful work and our place in the sun, in the meantime listen to life. True for those looking for a place in the sun, rewarding work, or words for the writers among us.

Today we'll read more with third grade students. Last week the teacher reminded one student until he has a million dollar book advance, it's best not to begin sentences with the word "And." The teacher is adamant and perhaps has already told Jack this a few times already.

After volunteering, I'll stop in at Fed Ex/ Kinko and fax the release form. Then it's a waiting game to see how my book circulates. "It's a learning adventure," said the locally owned bookstore person. There is much more to writing books than simply filling words on a page. Books take us places within their words and outside their chapters as we market our product. First we must set a price.

My brother in Philadelphia called last night. He reminds me to bring the t-shirt with the number sixty on it, worn initially at my parents anniversary party. Our oldest brother has a surprise party in less than two weeks. We will help him celebrate, although perhaps many don't look forward to turning a new decade. I'm ten years behind him.

The UPS delivery man thought we had a new camera. Some days it's much better than a picture. Instead we paint with words recorded for others to see what we've seen along the route. Or heard as in the case of my first book published, and most other books.

I will go to physical therapy later and hope my shoulder improves with twice daily exercise. We fit it into our routine, much like writing fits our day, often starting the day.

We write in morning while the rest of the world awakens. We write in the quiet of morning as a single airplane makes its way across the sky. I faxed my first book approval yesterday.

Later the publisher e-mails they will release it, publish my words and let the world read what we've written. Like children we send off into the world, we hope they will be accepted, successful. While we set the book's price, the reading public ultimately sets price and decides whether our words are worth purchasing. Still writing is done for the writer, we write for ourselves.

We read of heirs, murder and evidence in yesterday's third grade reading. Evidence which was definitive, irrefutable. I read through the third grade students reports on bridges.

Portland has many. One bridge, the oldest of its kind. Another literally overrides several smaller bridges. Suppose in some ways interstate freeways similarly bypass smaller roadways along their route.

The kids had drawn in the bridges alongside their three paragraphs of history, cost and current day passenger traffic. My friend Marilyn wasn't in. Wonder if she like several of the students has symptoms of the flu.

Next week I'll fly to Philadelphia and then drive to Vermont with an older brother. Today the Vice President says his family won't take commercial flights; it's too risky, as soon as someone sneezes, it exposes the aircraft. The airlines are quick in their response. Some in America still fly commercial, much of the electorate as it works out. Us, all of us, or at least those Americans lucky enough to travel by air.

We write as frogs echo outside and the house slowly awakens. We write with words, the progress of getting them in book form, regardless the time frame of publishers. They are backlogged as more people place their words on the page.

Today I have physical therapy at noon. I might try reading through *A Sibling Within* if time permits. I'd like to send this manuscript before leaving on vacation. There is still editing to do. The book is written yet we take out more with each edit. Sometimes we add a few sentences or a better word.

We have already told the story, yet we try telling it with less words, simpler language in a manner which flows. We write in early morning as breakfast cereal wrap twists and bagels are placed in the toaster.

We log what happens rooms away, what we plan to do in today's routine and where our writing leads. Writing often chooses its path, it writes itself if only we step aside. Let writing reveal the words, story told one morning at a time.

Some mornings there is more to log in, other days not so much. The excitement of receiving our first book one day, the next, ongoing routine. Last night I received an e-mail a college friend will be in town.

He will be in San Francisco in June. Trouble is, I'm in Portland. I've been here twenty years. Sometimes e-mails don't connect, so too within our writing.

Today starts a new month. I read through half of *A Sibling Within*. Midmorning, an insurance agent from Ohio calls. "I know you are busy," she says. "I'll keep it brief." Ten minutes later laments she always wanted to write. I remind her, her story waits and is as valid.

She no longer sells insurance, rather listens in on writing. "Write daily on the everyday," I tell her. "Start with the insurance person calling." Then go elsewhere to sit and write. Place yourself in a new setting. Weave everyday in as you write of another place and time.

She listens and later apologizes for interrupting. "I look forward to reading *A Sibling Within*," she says. The idea people leave yet are still beside us captures her imagination. She isn't so interested in *Jobless in Seattle*. I laugh thinking at least the title works although not so much sleepless, or jobless in Seattle, rather finding balance in life in spite where we are, what we do, or who we do it for.

I read further and then race across town for physical therapy. Today it is with Nancy. She finds my flexibility limited. Instead of the wall routine, she places me on the floor, on my back. We take it from there - slowly.

Each day her new exercise, a yoga position she offers, will help bring my body back in alignment. "It's about posture," she tells me. "Posture, and relaxing."

Once home, the answering machine blinks. It's the publishers and they require money before mailing the initial set of free books, posters and postcards. I order more books as they have a twenty percent off sale. Although the book order desk person has a British Columbia accent, he is now at their new headquarters in Indiana.

Later I mow the lawn. Madeline comes outside with telephone in hand. The property management guy needs money too.

First he wants an approval to update an apartment. My twenty year tenant passed away last month. Now the place needs an upgrade. It's the owner's unit and will sparkle after new carpet, countertops, plumbing and light fixtures.

"You upgrade one thing and the rest looks out of place," says the property manager. He gives me the lock box combination in case I want to see it before and then after upgrades.

We write of everyday and those days the telephone rings - often. One wanting to know about writing although selling insurance at the time. Another with caller ID from Indiana rerouted through British Columbia; a Canadian accent amid America's heartland. We write of remodeling living space, after the departure of long term tenants. His obituary read simply - "He was a musician."

Keeping it simple sometimes tells the story best. We understand there was music in their life; theirs and everyone else they come in contact with. Some days this contact is over the telephone, other days they activate our book and it appears online ready for sale.

This too adds to our day. It is one of those days and I mean this in a good way. I hope the turn of a calendar page starts something good.

Madeline tests for her violin. Three of them will perform and get graded later this morning. Then three neighboring schools will each hold a concert of their own. She is up early getting breakfast, dressed, and excited. Abby sits in the family room recliner watching cartoons. Yesterday they upgraded the television cables and now our television comes in much clearer, with additional channels.

We write in early morning, before the violin testing and cartoons. We mention the everyday, mowing of the grass and picking up of yard debris. Lately there is an increase of cigarette butts and shattered glass. It happens. Still I'm surprised as we've moved to a nicer community. Litter doesn't discriminate.

Last night a college friend e-mailed. He retired from the Air Force and now continues in much the same position as a civilian. He wrote of his two daughters. Years ago we didn't have much in common, perhaps as time goes on we have more to talk about.

Ironically, I spent four years in the military before college, he spends over twenty years after college.

Another e-mail introduces my new publishing assistant. Trafford is bought by Author Solutions. While printing remains on Vancouver Island, the processing of book orders moves to Indiana. A new location, a new contact for printing our books.

The birds sing outside as laundry whirls. The kids eat breakfast as mom hurries along their pace. We will drive a neighbor's child to the concert. One parent is out of town, the other has to work.

A younger brother e-mailed also yesterday. I'll stay with him while in town to celebrate our oldest brother's birthday. He works late shift and wonders if he has to take time off, the day I fly back. Think he will be able to do this en-route to his shift.

I read through the second half of *A Sibling Within*. Now twenty or so edit revisions to input and may call this book complete. No book is ever done, no story told in its entirety.

Still there is grammar, punctuation and flow to check before sending stories on to the publisher. They read easier and we hope tell a story; a story which captures readers attention early on and keeps them reading. We add in chirping birds, laundry and the breakfast cereal. Still this is background music to plot, there has to be a story underneath and weaved within.

Often we find these story threads, those seeds further along in writing. We begin and trust the process of logging in words. Weeks, months, sometimes years later, a story finds its way within our writing.

We write of the everyday. Most everyone relates to daily routine. Still it's what happens once we lose sight of the chirping birds which build story. What happens when we no longer hear those birds, laundry, cereal wrap or even distant airplanes. We write beyond life's distraction.

Today it is keeping early morning schedule so Madeline can be tested on her violin progress. It's Saturday morning and most would prefer sleeping in. The birds sing outside, maybe this month we will entice them to stay around awhile.

It's been a delayed spring, early May and we wear sweaters. With swine flu out of control, perhaps it's safe to travel with layers. First we will see how things play out for the sixth grade violin players.

Madeline is at a sleepover. Abby sleeps beside our bed on her couch cushion mattress. I was up late reading through *Twice Found Postcards*. I listened, hearing more of Oscar's story of escaping World War II. We met outside a dental clinic. He was staring at our Volkswagen Passat after I left from having my teeth cleaned.

He needs several fillings and an adjustment to his bridge, still he celebrates his luck landing on American soil. My book also follows neighbors bound for Hawaii. They too celebrate, perhaps like many celebrating once we set off on vacation, and not so much grateful within the everyday.

The main story line is set in Las Vegas. I write as I walk along miles of Las Vegas Boulevard. It's not my place in the sun, although there is much to distract. Las Vegas keeps many distracted - long term.

The violin testing goes well. The monitor is surprised lessons are held for seventy students at one time. Nonetheless she encourages my daughter and her two friends to continue playing.

"Buy books on violin music," she encourages "or find someone who's played a bit longer and learn from them." In essence, music is enjoyable and thus enjoy those moments of practice which build a lifetime of music.

Nina is my sixth grade daughter's height. Still music fills her life as she explains how to use more bow, start in unison, and being brave with our music. She later accompanies my daughter's trio on the piano. She happens to know the song. My guess, she plays many songs and perhaps several instruments. Music is part of Nina's life and she hopes it becomes a part of life for the children she tests.

Later we have a quick Mexican lunch before driving across town. "I've never gone this far down this road," says Abby. We walk through an apartment vacated by a twenty nine year tenant. He lived in the owners unit and kept it meticulous. Still the apartment shows its thirty years. We will return to see upgrades later in the month: new carpet, countertops, fixtures and life.

The space is there with a second living area and attached garage. When he passed away his obituary was short and to the point. It simply read, "Jim was a musician."

We should all die musicians. Or more apt, live as musicians. Better still, be musicians, people with music in our lives. In his own way he brought music to mine.

Melissa and Abby spend much of the afternoon watching Tori Spelling live: her jewelry sales, book signings, along with the everyday. "I was lonely," Melissa notes "while you were crowded."

Suppose marriages attract opposites. A dozen siblings force us to see the world differently. Many ask to write of this experience.

Writing is reaching for their voice, telling it in ours. Sometimes we are successful, on key like violins and cellos which played earlier in unison as parents listened. The conductor notes many are confident enough to watch him as they play during the concert. This is a good thing, more so in sixth grade, early in their life of music.

Today it rains. The winter winds will be back later tonight. The wind, hail and heavy rain were here for much of the past few days. Still I managed to sit outside and edit a bit of *A Sibling Within*. Later I took a nap.

The rains and wind had electricity blink throughout the day and night. I went to bed late only to be awaken by my clock radio alarm. Fifteen minutes later, it blares once again. Neither were at the six am setting, rather awakening me at midnight and again minutes later. Thus I took a nap midway through yesterday.

"You got up in a bad mood," notes my wife. We had to be somewhere early and this adds to my edginess. Madeline is at a sleep over so morning is not routine. It hurries along nonetheless.

Two days ago my younger brother e-mailed perhaps while in town I could sort through some of my parent's attic. It's their attic yet I have a crate of junk up there; paperwork from military, college and life.

We stash it for another day, which leads to years, even decades. Some papers important at the time, now less relevant. Still I will try going up there weather permitting. The floorboards are also a challenge.

We write of neighbor cars speeding off to work, outbursts of our child sleeping rooms away and the otherwise morning quiet. Today nothing is on the schedule. Tomorrow, another Bible study session. The day after is busy.

I volunteer in Abby's third grade classroom, then physical therapy and home to pack. Maybe I'll take along an extra suitcase as there is an attic to unload.

Madeline was honored Sunday for her altar service. Her slumber party was fun. They play several games. One a word they can not use the entire day. Another places M&M's in their mouths two at a time. They can only eat them once they find matching ones.

Another game involves a celebrity name on their backs and guessing by a series of comments from their friends. Games at sixth grade slumber parties. It beats waking up with an off schedule clock radio alarm.

This weather continues off key. Early May and we have hail. Sweater weather as we close in on the end of school year. Many are closed down due to swine flu.

Even the Catholic church takes precautions by no longer offering wine. They also ask us not to shake hands with those around us. The swine flu is pandemic, affecting most every country across the world.

Meanwhile my first book has been released from publishing house Trafford. Still I have a hard time finding it anywhere else on the web. Maybe this week it too will spread, first by online bookstores and then around the world. Books circulate in their own perfect time, while others merely make it to our personal bookshelves.

Too many others stay lodged inside, we don't take time to pencil in words, our story or another's told through us. Writers make time to spend with their words. They log in the hospital visits, violin recitals, the everyday. Even those days of winter wind and hail amid the early part of May. Keep a sweater and umbrella handy.

Today the kids sleep in as laundry whirls. I turn on my den light yet it seems dark. The overnight storm clouds must still be blocking outside light.

I read through the beginning and last pages of a book initially titled *Twice Found Postcards* to my wife last night. She asks if I wrote the remainder of the book, the inside pages to the story. It's been written and edited several times. Still, I'm not sure of the title.

She wonders if perhaps there are two many people and settings in the story. The story works well enough, it's just the title can be better. A book's title is one of the hooks to get people reading and curious enough to purchase our writing.

A good title writes the song. Suppose this is no different for books. Some start out titled, this one lingers in that department.

Yesterday, I received an e-mail from my new author assistant. They recently merged with a larger company, thus a juggling of staff. I also received a login to review progress of our books through the printing production line. It also tracks royalty payments. Ideally this gives us one more reason to log on our computers.

Today I will input more revisions on *Twice Found Postcards*. Then I'll print and may share it with Marilyn at the elementary school. Or maybe I'll let it simmer for awhile and then send it to the publisher.

Writing takes awhile placing words on the page. Stories come to us in the everyday. We overhear a funny phrase or our child gives us a line of their own. We integrate the everyday into a story of back then. Mixing up characters and dialogue amid the mix of timeframes.

Fictions allows this and more. We write creating any story which wants to be recorded. We don't leave without our story. We don't leave without their story. We hope the reading public recognizes a part of themselves in stories we write down.

Today is laundry day. I'll start to pack as well. My brother's sixtieth birthday party is this weekend. I'll fly to Philadelphia midweek, on his actual birth date. Then I'll drive to Vermont with another brother.

Still another brother e-mailed last week perhaps I could work on my parents' attic. It's raining here and on the east coast. Let's wait for warmer and dryer weather before unpacking this crate of memories.

We store things for another day, invariably it is years later before we get the chance to look through our storage boxes. Many are school textbooks, while others are papers we wrote ourselves; a generation ago of term papers and accounting tests.

It's early morning rain as laundry whirls and the kids sleep a final few minutes. Tomorrow Abby sees the high school kids perform Suessical. I have a physical therapy appointment, although she wants me to join her and her classmates.

I will read with Abby's third grade classmates and then go to physical therapy. The medical appointment moved up a day since tomorrow I fly to Philadelphia. Tomorrow is my oldest brother's birthday.

He turns sixty and I turn fifty later this fall. Late summer my youngest sister turns thirty nine. Thus I'm in the middle, as we age, celebrating milestones - those birthdays in between.

We write of daily writing, traffic, and the weather outside. We mention medical appointments and our volunteer efforts. Ideally they matter to the kids we come in contact with. Reading begins in grade school and continues through life. So too with learning, a lesson learned early in grade school. Still learning is facilitated, we must do it for ourselves.

I was on a roll yesterday inputting more edit revisions on *Twice Found Postcards*. Mid afternoon friends call to use the computer. Later I went to a weekly Bible study. Both didn't allow time to input all the revisions. I wanted to finish with this book before leaving on vacation; leaving on vacation and giving a copy to Marilyn to read through.

My first book is ready. Still I don't want to share the first copy with anyone. I'll wait to give her a copy once the initial free order gets here later next month.

Then I'll take one to the Jantzen Beach hotel bookshelf. I'll drop one off at Goodwill. I'll place one at a friend's retirement community. Then a copy at the beach bookstore and their library.

We not only write our books, we must market them. Still by strategically placing them within family, friends and special locations, we hope the reading public enjoys our work. They in turn place them with family, friends and their own special locations.

We each have our favorite reading nooks and bookshelves. I'll also submit a short note to Barnes & Noble explaining how my book is special. Special or unique, is what the booksellers require. I'll tell them my book listens.

My book listens, this should get their attention and ideally my book circulating. I priced it at $12.25, this is Christmas for the rest of us. May it be gifted often.

A Sibling Within will build on this momentum, at least that's my hope. I'll price it at $24.07, twenty four seven - twenty four hours seven days a week. Pricing books can be a fun exercise in itself. This book recaps the Tenderloin hotel lobby group, my sister's tragic accident and life amid a dozen siblings. They were around twenty four seven.

Twice Found Postcards will sell for twenty one dollars. This is a book on Las Vegas. Tongue in cheek, we price books accordingly. It's a book about receiving postcards found years later; twice sent postcards, even after people have long since passed. They don't leave without their story.

None of us do, still not everyone writes their own down. Sometimes it's those left behind who pen the words in Oregon early morning rain. Before the routine of daily life begins. Before volunteering, physical therapy and a flight to Philadelphia. Before the sixtieth birthday celebration.

I am up earlier than usual, today I fly to Philadelphia. I will be on east coast time for a few days. My oldest brother turns sixty today, although his surprise party is this weekend. We continue to have forty degree weather - and rain. Back east is also having a cold, wet and late start to summer.

I've packed accordingly. No Birkenstocks and shorts this time, rather I take along a raincoat and sweaters. The physical therapy has helped. I have one more session and then continue the stretches and exercises on my own. I also spend time with Marilyn before volunteering with third grade students.

Yesterday we were to find stray sentences. Abby later explains the thinking behind this. Still as a college graduate, who writes no less, I find the third grade exercise a challenge. I tell the kids as much.

Later I input more pages of edits. *Twice Found Postcards* is almost done. Yesterday I was finally able to word the title. I knew postcards and perhaps the word within would be in it. Still it took awhile to title this book.

It took a trip to the airport, meeting someone outside a dental clinic and years spent with my mother in law to write this story. Still like much of our writing, we spend time bringing it into the present and choose active verbs. We delete the "get to's, have to's," and "so to speak." We get rid of "was, is" and words ending in "ing." We replace them with active verbs and active voice. Our voice speaks throughout writing, we write in ours reaching for theirs.

Writing daily captures those moments which add to and build story. Late last night Madeline had a fever. Today Melissa will drive me to the airport and then call work. She will also call Madeline's school. We write daily of our travel plans, household's health and weather outside and across the country.

Tomorrow we will drive from Philadelphia to Vermont. There is heavy traffic midway passing through New York City. Still with forecasted rain, it will be an even longer drive.

It's been awhile since I drove this route and I look forward to the scenery. It also allows a ten hour visit with my brother. It's been awhile since traveling together. He visited often when I lived in New York City years ago.

Today, Portland is home; Portland with the enviable quality of life, even if weather seems off this year. Record snow around the holidays and now the delayed summer. I've still a few things to pack, then it's off to the airport. Perhaps this swine flu keeps people off airplanes and hope it's not a full flight so I can stretch out.

I considered buying my brother sixty of something. Still I doubt he needs M&M's, pencils or anything else in this quantity. My hope this surprise party is just that.

He will be surprised indeed as it coincides with Mother's Day. Only later will he realize something is amiss as more and more people show up at his home. More is better in this case; more people, not so much years on our personal calendars.

Today we leave Philadelphia for Princeton, on through New York City, Albany and the green mountains of Vermont. We will stop for a quick breakfast early along the route. The east is humid, although today is much nicer than the computer lead us to believe just days before.

We write early morning, while we drive through New Jersey in search of the New York State Thruway which leads through six million acres of the Adirondack National Park. Lots of red ledges border otherwise green vistas in the distance.

Philadelphia had a beautiful sunset as we left the airport. My flight from Chicago is delayed two hours. I am lucky to reschedule on an earlier flight delayed as well. I land in Philadelphia a half hour late.

My brother waits after considering which terminal United uses. I read through signs on corridor walls as I search for the baggage area. Flying into unfamiliar airports is disorienting. We will surprise our oldest brother on Sunday. This weekend is also Mother's Day. We celebrated a few weekends early having a brunch at a Columbia riverfront hotel.

Madeline fights a flu. The doctor says it is just a passing bug and wait it out. Meanwhile Abby goes to school and mom stays home to watch Madeline. They planned to go to movies and have fun while I'm in Vermont celebrating my brother's sixtieth birthday, Mother's Day and spending time with a younger brother.

We bypass New York City and most of it's bridges by driving a more circular route west of the metropolitan area. It is longer yet an easier drive. I plan to help my brother drive part of the way. Vacation, a time to see new landscapes with family and friends.

The airlines greet us with a service fee of fifteen dollars per checked bag. "I'll carry it on board," I tell them. Luckily later all I have is carry on and am able to get an earlier scheduled connecting flight at O'Hare. It too is delayed.

Today, flying often means a delay, overcharge and less service all around. Not even peanuts are offered. I searched the Portland airport for a trinket for my oldest brother. What do you buy someone turning sixty? A cutting board which reads, "I'm running so far behind, I think I'm first." Being oldest, he often is first.

Magnets and food are tourist priced for those hurrying through airports. Vendors hope we make impulse purchases. Realistically they won't see us again soon. We rush through airports, only to be met with delay and stringent rules asking we carry three ounce liquids or less.

My day began pouring contact lens solution, saving the remaining three ounces. We write of everyday and what starts our day. We write within daily routine and the non-routine which is modern day flight.

The fog comes through trees this morning as we awaken. Birds sing outside as traffic passes in the distance. The drive to Vermont yesterday went easily. Rather than predicted rain, we have clear skies for much of the route. At Albany, New York there are showers and Olive Garden in the Latham suburb proves elusive.

We'd had lunch there years ago. "It's at Exit 9," says the tollbooth person. "Latham is at this exit." Later another person says, "Find Wolffe Road, it's ten minutes from here - a left, another left and it's on your right side." We find Wolffe Road yet there is no Olive Garden restaurant.

The Albany airport is nearby which I remember being close to this restaurant. We later leave the Albany area after a half hour delay without lunch. McDonalds further up the line suffices with its chicken wraps and cappuccino - vanilla cappuccino.

We drive onto my sister's home. She lives in the city I went to grade and high school. Short of two years in junior high, I was bussed daily to this city. Thus I am more familiar with its layout, although I looked forward to a leisurely lunch on the drive up. A chance to get out of the car and have a full meal. Eating, we will do lots of this while vacationing in Vermont.

Last night my sister served lasagna and strawberry shortcake. Later playing cards and visiting with my parents, we have cake, ice cream and a wedge of brownie. Instead of cappuccino, it's beer this time.

The birds and traffic continue outside the upstairs window. A floor below, the ongoing breakfast chatter. We have waffles, strawberries and Vermont maple syrup. Green Mountain coffee tops off breakfast.

Earlier I called my younger brother. He doesn't answer. I e-mail although his address is refused. I delete my e-mail and call him once again. Vermont often the backdrop to delay. We write in early morning alongside the outdoor chirp, or above breakfast conversation a floor below.

Last night there were a few stories on keeping the local church cemetery groomed. My sister is responsible for mowing. My oldest brother helps cut back several trees which fell during a recent storm.

He says my sister has "hundreds of people below her" as she works her way through the cemetery. "I never get a complaint," she replies. "Fences around cemeteries protect us from those dying to get in," my youngest brother chimes in. So goes an evening visiting family, playing cards, cribbage and eating.

Today I will try sorting through some articles placed in my parents attic. It's sat out there for decades and perhaps no longer worth storing. I will sort through and hope to throw more away during this trip to Vermont. All trips to Vermont are a trip back in time. Time goes on regardless where we might spend weekends. We write of everyday, the birds outside even the early morning fog.

There was a blanket of fog last night driving back to my sister's from my parents home. A full moon visible within various pockets of fog, along the rough and winding roads. Up and down they curve along infamous knolls of the rustic New England state amid early summer fog.

Today it has cleared and by days end I hope more has cleared from my parents attic. We sort ongoing. Some days we throw out part of our collection. The parts no longer worth saving, storing, or valuable decades later.

The Vermont summer continues, it rains. It rains this morning. It rained yesterday - hail before that. Some areas receive golf ball size hail.

Birds pass by outside, a cardinal flew by yesterday while having breakfast of waffles and Green Mountain coffee. My sister often has a full house. Her busy kitchen and full pantry play in keeping family around, if not housed and fed while on vacation.

Across the road from my parents is a property listed with eleven bedrooms. Our neighbor's wife passed away a few years ago and now the family's summer retreat is for sale. It comes with over one hundred twenty five acres. "That isn't enough to farm viably," my father notes.

I offer someone might be more in the market for a hobby farm; a place to spend time in seclusion after a busy week in the city, in the midst of people, in the midst of life. Someone will come along looking for just such a place, whether there is a gourmet kitchen or nearly a dozen bedrooms. Perhaps a bed and breakfast will surface across the street from my parents home.

Yesterday my youngest brother walked across the road with a lamb in his arms. My parents and a few siblings are surprised to hear the lamb bleat. My parents note it has grown a lot since seeing it weeks earlier at my father's eighty eighth birthday party.

Earlier we went to a local restaurant for lunch. A family table for eleven as it were, five are not available due to family obligations, work or not being contacted. Some keep themselves out of the loop, unplugged when off work, whether they have luxury of one hundred twenty five acres surrounding them or not.

I sort through the attic midday. I spend the afternoon looking through college and army material. Books, textbooks and clothes will go to Goodwill. I scan through check registers of the army and college years.

I kept pay receipts from all four years of service. I also stashed stuff upon moving from New York City. There are maps, papers and travel expense logs from working at a bank there in the mid 1980's. I throw out hundreds of business cards which read auditing with one of the major banks.

I sort and repack stuff ready for Goodwill as it rains outside. Several crates of paper are ready to burn. Later I look through my upstairs bedroom with more pictures, papers and a manual typewriter.

I read through my mother's 1977 diary. There are three of them in the dresser bottom drawer. Probably not an accident these years 1977 through 1979 are there. I joined the service in 1977 and enjoy reading through how my parents days fill during this year of change: graduation, army, birth of a niece and a nephew.

My mother also has a pair of pants, plaid from nearly thirty years ago waiting. "Here, I think these are yours," as I fill a duffle bag to cart off the remaining memories of my parents home. I leave with a duffle filled with a tapestry from my grandparents, books, notebooks from high school and college. A suitcase the airlines will charge fifteen dollars yet holds much more value. I pack what remains of the army years, college and life long ago.

My sister later asks if I cried while sifting through decade old belongings and memories. What's important is whether she cries later as she reads of my experience. I'll place her beside us as I sort through my parents attic, with Vermont cold summer rain hitting the metal roof.

It's not necessarily a sad episode, still perhaps a rite of passage. In any case an afternoon full of story seeds. Even my mother in law crosses my mind as a birthday card from her drops to the floor. It mentions racing through hell and purgatory to send it off in time.

Still she spends eternity in heaven, if not in our memory. This might get readers teary eyed yet the sadness has passed and onward to the future and all it holds. Let's hope this includes sunshine before the end of the calendar May page.

I write this morning outside Stowe, Vermont. Sun has just broke the horizon. Radio airs from Montreal and tells of a local Alzheimer project and an escaped orangutan in Australia.

Downstairs, my brother moves through his kitchen. We will have breakfast at McDonalds. The VonTrapp Lodge would be a nicer setting and much more expensive if not leisurely paced meal. Will save this for lunch at Best Western near the Burlington airport.

Yesterday we toasted our oldest brother. He turned sixty this past week. A new decade for him. I'll turn fifty later this summer, too soon for any of us to begin new decades. Even weekends go by too quickly, weekends celebrating with: family, cards, jokes and telling of our everyday. It gives us more to write about.

Midway through explaining my recent visits to the physical therapist, I suggest perhaps it's due to the increase in writing lately. I tell several of my siblings gathered around one of two dining room tables I write.

My daughter Madeline said she shivered as they introduced her to her new school classmates. Like this I suppose as I tell them about my book, my books, all three. I say the first is on listening. This should get them talking.

Later we talk of marketing in America. Even books sell, not necessarily because of their words, rather effective marketing. One wants to know if she is mentioned, as I say the second deals with family and our position within nuclear birth family and the greater world community of siblings.

One sister knows someone within the Barnes & Noble hierarchy. Another hints Oprah might help, several are ready for that event. Writing gets words on the page and ideally our reading audience talking, even siblings those present as we celebrate family member milestones, and those left behind.

My brother has four of his grandsons blow out his birthday candles. I watch from across the table. Vermont is backdrop to the early years. It is setting to the early parts of my life and often those moments spent with family in celebration. Sometimes we throw in our ongoing activities, those they are mentioned within.

We write early morning regardless where we are. We write in dens at home, in upstairs guest bedrooms in northern Vermont or airports during a stopover on our way back cross country. We write of everyday and those days filled with tables of conversation. One sister notes there are a dozen conversations going on simultaneously. This is before she starts telling her tale of the time when...

She is at the wrong airport. She has her children, luggage yet at the last minute, stranded at the airport across town. Another time when tears fall in the back pew and again later at a park bench.

She ends this story by mentioning it rains outside. "It rains - hard" she says. Sometimes it does through life's downpours and yet like a melody it moves us. Life moves, especially when turning new decades, as we celebrate those milestones, memories and music along the way.

The laundry starts. I've unpacked clothes from this past weekend's trip back east. I'll look through real estate catalogues later, those found outside the breakfast restaurant in Stowe. Stoneybrook, I think it was called. My brother and I enjoyed a leisurely breakfast and then drove by newer and still being built condominiums at the base of Mount Mansfield.

Then we drove to the VonTrapp Lodge and walked for an hour through forested trails before stopping in to see a bit of the lodge interior: the pub, and lobby. There are various libraries, dens tucked within, others oversized sunrooms.

It is postcard scenery and weather to match. Afterwards we walk a bit of the Lake Champlain waterfront, a boardwalk along part of downtown Burlington. It is a scenic view there too with calm waters of Lake Champlain and the Adirondack Mountains of New York off in the western horizon. Lake Champlain accessible to the Atlantic via the Hudson River; accessible to the Great Lakes via the St Lawrence Seaway.

We stop for lunch before heading to the airport. I fly back through Washington DC, on time if not having to be searched, padded down. The Burlington airport keeps it green, requiring cash only at the Green Mountain Coffee café. It is an interesting exchange, as I don't spend cash, and wonder how they get away requiring cash only. "We are short a telephone line," the clerk explains.

At Washington DC weather turns, we are delayed an hour due to the incoming rainstorm. We sit beside runways waiting for the storm to pass. A half hour delay going east, now an hour delay returning west.

The laundry fills with water. It's early morning as I'm still on eastern time, in my den logging in today and a bit of yesterday, last week specifically. I think my oldest brother was surprised to see most of us in town celebrating his turning six decades. Looking through my desk for writing paper, I spot the past week's mail. There are also two cardboard boxes. Melissa and the kids said UPS had not made their delivery.

Beside my desk, next to other daily mail sit two boxes of my book on listening. It's a welcome surprise. While home I mention I wrote a book or three.

Thus the recent shoulder trouble as I've been on the laptop computer more. I said my first book was on listening. This should get them talking. It does, and they probably continue as they wait for copies I'll mail them later today.

Still as I told my siblings and family members gathered, it's not so much what we say in books, rather what others tell themselves as they read along. This, and no one has a corner on the story market; each of our stories as valid as the next. Some scream with an army of publicists, still I'd like to think the best written stories end atop the bestseller list.

While on stopover at Dulles airport I ask the Borders Bookstore salesperson for ideas to place my book on their store shelves. Consignment is one way to do it locally. As for getting within the entire chain, write a letter to Ann Arbor, Michigan.

This is where those chain wide decisions are made. It gives me something to think about. Ideally my books do the same; the first and those which follow. The washing machine now spins a week's laundry as an airplane climbs in the sky.

The heat is on again this morning although the calendar reads mid May. Today I volunteer in Abby's third grade classroom. This will end soon as volunteer schedule is usually a month short of the school year.

Today Marilyn who proof read my second book draft, gets a copy of my first published one on listening to life. During the school year she keeps asking about the book's printing process. "Where's that book about finding our place in the sun?" she asks. Today this book is ready to be read by Marilyn. I also throw in a few bookmarks and postcards, marketing aides to our writing.

Marilyn is an only child yet doesn't travel life alone. I send five copies to a sister in Vermont. Another two to family members, one in Baltimore, the other, Hartford. I include a note, "Enjoy you're in it!" I'd written this months ago, hoping one day to insert this into one of my books.

This day passes. Now will the day of having my books move off the shelf, the bestsellers shelf come to pass. Time will tell. After the hour at school, I'll drop off a few more copies of my book. One at a retirement community where Ms. Pond lives. She turns ninety seven this August and is mentioned toward the book's end.

A few copies will go to Goodwill. Never know who browses their bookshelves. Another will be on the shelf at a hotel across town. They have a book exchange for guests. Again this group of people travel and I hope take it along for the ride, moving our message, our books along with them.

Yesterday there were two boxes of books and promotional material next to my desk. I was in Vermont when UPS makes this delivery. My wife and kids were successful in keeping it a surprise. I too have been asking if they'd seen my book, the one about looking for meaningful work and our place in the sun.

Birds chirp outside as the shadow of my writing hand moves across the page. Last night we had a Mexican dinner across town. Our friend is back from London. She is in town to see her father. The fun part of writing is telling the story.

Still there is a story in moving our words off the bookshelves. I'd hoped to drop off a copy at my brother's in Philadelphia while home celebrating our oldest brother's sixtieth.

Instead his apartment had one too many bookshelves and perhaps it would be awhile before he found my book. Books should circulate. His apartment holds the entire store. A minimalist would panic before reaching the top stair.

We write in early morning, during the quiet of day. We write before planning our route. Today it is a stop at school and then driving around town to distribute my book. Some places will get bookmarks only with gist of the book and how to order it online.

Selling is selling I tell the kids as we back out the garage. Some sell wine, others real estate. Still others sell books, words written and later marketed. Ideally they sell themselves down the road. In other words, our books mean something, say something to others. They get, understand our words, story - us.

I give my book to Marilyn. We are in the elementary school atrium waiting to volunteer. Today I will time their reading speed and see if they can beat the clock with multiplication tables. Time changes their pace and challenges their concentration. It's a fun morning as I watch them count aloud, on their fingers or look askew waiting for the multiplication table of six to materialize.

Marilyn wants to know about the birthday party back in Vermont. "How are your parents? How is your brother and family?" It was a few days of celebration, I tell her.

Earlier I gave my book on finding balance in life to my wife's college roommate. I hand a book to her along with the book's own postcard and bookmark. "You don't know how to market," she tells me.

Later I drive to Jantzen Beach hoping to place one of my books on their book exchange shelves. The hotel corridor only has six books this morning. I angle mine in so people will see it as they round the hotel corridor.

I stuff a bookmark in my sleeve as I plan to place it in a book at the other end of the hotel. There are two sets of bookcases for guests to exchange books. There is a conference in the front lobby. I walk in and there are tables of Indian crafts.

The front table is the United States Post Office. I laugh thinking why does the Post Office need to market itself. Later I meet Steve, who explains many people don't fully use the postal services while others head for Federal Express or use United Parcel Service.

We chat awhile. He mentions his brother in Florida. I tell him I just wrote a book parts set in Florida and had strategically placed it on the hotel bookshelf.

He mentions Bert Sperling is a band member and asks if I have any books available. As it works out, I have a carload. I give him two. Goodwill also gets two.

I tell him about my other books. *A Sibling Within* piques his interest. This one resonates the most with me. Suppose this is why I get that reaction from others. "When is that book available?" they ask.

I drive further to place a few more books. A bookmark falls from my sleeve. It's a strange day indeed.

Hours ago I'm told I don't know what I'm doing regarding the selling of books. Minutes ago I get chills. The brother in the same Florida city. Bert Sperling, the Portland resident who writes of the best places to live is a band member of the person I'm talking to. I drive further thinking how serendipitous life can be. It changes in a flash, depending on who we meet.

Books allow others to meet us - the odd juxtaposition of intimate conversation from afar. Still readers join our conversation if writing is successful. Stories go to the heart of the matter. Fiction described as shared emotional experience.

At home I put my coat away as my bookmark falls from my sleeve. Today I literally had something up my sleeve. Like the forgotten bookmark, sometimes life has it's own share of surprises. Some days they are wonderful surprises.

Later after dinner with friends, I hand a book to another friend, Marilyn. She enjoys reading through a few pages and says to place it here, there, even the airport. "What are you waiting for?" she asks. I say her daughter said much the same earlier this morning.

Still my boxes of books were delivered only two days ago. The book will sell on the internet. Word of mouth sells too. My youngest sister e-mails. She places an order online. I hope she enjoys it as she is mentioned early on.

Just now the rain starts. It's been a cold wet spring. We write amid the wet weather and book marketing. We write of everyday routine, and twist along the route. Some thrill and qualify for heart map stories. Those days stand out and all future ones because of those particular days.

Yesterday I left a copy in a local retirement community lobby. I signed it with a note, "Enjoy you're in it, Ms. Pond." She is toward the end of my book, and no doubt life as she turns ninety seven in three months.

I had my last physical therapy session yesterday. I leave behind a copy in their waiting area along with the assorted magazines. Who knows who will pass through? Reading changes lives. It's finding a random book and taking the author's message further.

Much like life, those serendipitous moments build each of our own lives. The people we meet who change us. Ideally down the road we become one of those "people met who change us." In other words, we mentor someone. Each of us has something to share.

Writers share their words, their experiences. Teachers - their lesson plans. Photographers may see or frame pictures different and give us a copy of their captured moment. Each of us has a different start in life and few lives follow a parallel route. We take each day as it comes. Still some are more memorable, either the day brings someone special in our path, or we celebrate alongside as they turn a new decade.

Yesterday I bought more office supplies. I leave with more pens, envelopes and yellow sticky notes. It's a thrill to jot, "Enjoy, you're in it," within the first few pages of my book.

Reading of familiar settings is exciting.

Reading of familiar people even more so.

Reading of ourselves is what writing is about. We listen in on life. We write of others yet invariably place ourselves within the story too.

We travel with our story characters. We are there with them, and hope future readers ride along as they read further. Reading takes us places even if we spend the day home in our dens. Writing does much the same. Today I wonder if my book will move from the store shelves.

Listening to life theme resonates with many. Perhaps it is a timely message at graduation: new jobs, relocations and beginning our work lives. Still even those require we listen to our strengths, talents and interests. Not so much an outside world of parents, pay scales or prestige, rather listening to what makes our life work.

What rewards us? How does our life make a difference? To make a difference for others, our life has to be personally rewarding. Following our passion is how it is often phrased. Listening works too, as my wife says, "It's called listening."

Writing books is time consuming. "How long did it take to write?" is often one of the first questions people ask. Still books take a lifetime to write. We draw from a lifetime of experience.

So too for work, the successful ones integrate their work into their everyday. They place themselves right in the middle and go from there. Some days we ask for help in getting our message across. "Is this what the world needs?" we ask.

An airplane climbs overhead as birds chirp outside and kids sleep in. It's early morning on a weekend. Today I will input a few final revisions to *A Sibling Within*. Then it's one edit away from sending to the printers. That's the hope, and one day reality.

I also read through *Twice Found Postcards* yesterday. Last night I asked Melissa and the kids for title ideas. This book too is written, although the title could be better. It will happen. No doubt like the sound of my pen this morning or the overhead airplane, title too will stream in.

In a moment it will be titled. Still I wait for that moment. For some reason this particular book which wrote quickly takes longer in finding a title. All books reveal themselves at their own pace. They write themselves on their own terms. We start in the middle and go from there.

I mail three copies of my first book. One to a friend I met while living in New York City. He wonders what I write. I place a yellow post it note inside with the "Enjoy, you're in it." I also send the first few pages of my second book, the one I e-mailed him about earlier last year. The one on how people leave, yet stay by our side ongoing.

I also send a copy to a college roommate's mom. Publicity is about placing our work in the right person's hand. She knows people. The third copy is mailed to more family. Ideally it is a message which resonates with many, perhaps timely at graduation. Listening helps at every stage in life, more so as people set off in new careers or search for a locale to call home.

I also stop into Powells, the United States' largest private bookstore. I leave a copy with the information desk. They will get back to me if they are interested. There are multiple buyers, sorted by book category. I expect someone sitting in a room with a sign above their door which reads, "Purchasing." Its million book inventory requires they be more organized and diversified.

I return to the underground parking lot looking for my car. Similar to my book earlier looking for a slot on the multilevel bookstore shelves. Each room a different color, dependent on subject matter.

We write in early morning. Some mornings our pen is louder than others. This morning it squeaks. Perhaps it will run out of ink soon, or its spring is loose. Either way, I literally hear my pen as it makes its way across the page.

The shadow of a schnauzer moves across the page in unison. We write despite distractions outside our den window and those on our writing page. We write logging in each days events, even those which eventually move our books.

First we must write those words down and phrase our passing days accordingly. We write as birds sing outside while kids sleep inside. We listen in on writing and hope future readers hear what we heard.

We take readers along with us. Today my world came crashing down. It's no doubt an omen of better days ahead. I've had a world map stuck on my den wall for some time. Today all that remains is blue and white glue drops on the wall. The world map is curled up on the floor.

I spent most of yesterday inputting more edits to *A Sibling Within*. It's the thirteenth time I read through the manuscript. Melissa reads through to chapter seven of my book on listening to life. She says she enjoys it with a bit of surprise in her voice. A "Who would of thunk?" kind of expression. We write and sooner or later our words say something. Sometimes they surprise others, spouses and maybe even ourselves.

Granted I wrote *A Sibling Within,* still I too enjoy reading the book I envisioned years ago. Today I will take out more of the parts that aren't relevant or those parts which even I don't care to read through. Yesterday I wrote Barnes & Noble. They ask what makes our book unique or special. I tell them mine listens. I'll tell Costco the same later today as I package a book for them. It's a timely message anytime, especially at graduation.

Listening works most anytime in life and perhaps makes life easier if not fuller. We listen as we write, read and live day to day.

We went to lunch with a neighbor yesterday. She too receives a copy of my first published book.

I don't include a note, "Enjoy, you're in it," even though she is weaved throughout the story. Early on she is in Las Vegas listening to Gladys Knight live. I'm in my den for the early part of the book listening to Gladys on my cassette disk player.

We write of daily events, what music plays in the background and even what no longer hangs on our walls. Yesterday I read we should leave one wall empty. A blank wall allows the eye to travel. In other words it makes a room more expansive, not having too many things to focus in on.

Perhaps this is part of the reason we enjoy a day at the beach. There is no obstruction in the horizon. Waves mesmerize yet the fact we can see forever changes things. We are taken away as there is less distraction, rather the ocean attracts us to linger and look into the distance, the horizon.

This morning it's a blank wall except for a few straggling drops of glue. While home last week to celebrate my oldest brother's sixtieth, I rummaged through the attic. I took a duffle bag back to Portland.

One item is a couple of deer on a blanket which for years hung on my grandparent's den wall. I also have a glass maple leaf dish from them. Mere tokens, yet they hold sentimental memories of people who've passed on. Without them we wouldn't be here - literally. They were my father's parents.

We write in the early morning den before the world awakens. Sometimes the world comes crashing down overnight and we start anew by replacing our world maps. Other times The World is docked downtown. Good days must be just ahead. A world of wonderful events. Maybe I'll replace this map with my grandparent's carpet of deer.

It's early morning, the kids are still asleep. Madeline was up earlier, coughing and reaching for a glass of water. Later she will see her pediatrician to find out what is going on. She has a field trip to the ocean Thursday. Would not want her to miss a highlight of her sixth grade school year, including a boat ride off the Newport coast.

Yesterday we spoke of God and his love. Love is God's message. I asked if anyone knew what God meant. I say it starts with the letter, "L." A first grade student blurts, "Lucas, God is Lucas."

Apparently he is over enthusiastic about his younger brother. The adults in the room laugh - out loud. Later, I tell the kid he makes many laugh with his comment. "It's all about Lucas," his mom adds.

Sometimes we don't get the response we expect, even if we give clues. Later a former boss's wife comes over and introduces herself. A familiarity, as though she already knows me without us having personally spoken. I worked with her husband for several years.

I spent much of yesterday taking out the, "writing is" and "get to's." We write at a fast clip and sometimes we are able to use those sentences. Other times we rework them, or discard them altogether.

Summer is here. Over eighty degrees this past weekend. Even the air conditioner kicked on several times. Meanwhile Madeline coughs. She lost a few teeth last week and now coughs. Maybe it is simply allergies as everything blooms this time of year.

They went to a movie yesterday. They said the movie was made out of clay. I stayed home and read through *A Sibling Within*. It takes time to write, even longer to write something which looks easy to write. We edit and one day are happy with the words, the story that remains.

"Keep the story, the everyday routine," my wife says. Even discussing writing is sometimes difficult. To me the everyday is the backdrop to story writing. It is not the story itself. I write and my wife tells me how. Ideally future readers enjoy our words, cadence, and story. The better stories are their story, one which resonates with them.

Thus we begin writing of ourselves and invariably write of others. Perhaps this is part of the reason people enjoy reading. They see themselves in someone else's words.

Maybe this is the stuff my wife says to delete. Still if we write story continuously, people tire of that narrative. Thus I find it's better to occasionally break and bring in the everyday. The everyday familiar yet unique or special to each of us.

The kids sleep in as late as possible. Later I will add lunch money to Abby's account. She tells me she is having hot lunch for the remainder of the year. Took awhile yet she finally figures out hot lunches are often better than a cold sandwich. Maybe it is because Madeline is under the weather and Abby would have to make her own cold sandwich.

It rains this morning. The birds are awake as laundry whirls from across the house. Madeline has a sinus infection. Last week she lost two teeth. Now she is on antibiotics. I input the last of my second edit on *Twice Found Postcards*. Later I read through the first half. I enjoy the story thus far, even though I wrote it.

My wife reads through the first ten pages. Early on she is in tears. "Phrase it this way," she later suggests. "Tell them that." Writing places readers in our setting, while using our voice to tell them a story.

Thus it's difficult when someone tells us how our voice should sound, or maybe even what to say. There is reason not every one writes. Even those who attempt to place stories to the page are challenged; once by our editing mind, and later by second readers.

Still most stories get translated and thus never so much what we say, or even write down, rather what the reader hears and takes away from the story. Thus the adage to write for those who, "get" us. Otherwise it is a futile attempt to write for all audiences. They won't connect regardless what we write, what we tell them, or even how we phrase it.

Suppose an analogy is having the world agree on one particular piece of art or even song. There is a reason for multiple radio stations. We each have a different rhythm reflected in our words, stories and how we write them.

The kids sleep in a few more minutes as the washing machine adds more water. They both have student council this morning. Maybe Madeline will stay home. She was sick last night. The medication zaps her energy.

I met a neighbor at the mailbox. We hadn't seen each other in months. She had been to Seattle over the weekend to see a few baseball games. I tell her about my shoulder, my brother's sixtieth birthday and everyday life.

We have mailbox clusters and those in subdivisions meet neighbors as we sort through daily mail. Yesterday there was a birthday party invitation for a six year old. Also an invitation to my nephew's wedding later this July in Vermont.

We write in the day's activity and what is in our mailbox. Today we'll meet friends for dinner. They are in town to see their father who is at a care facility; a convalescent facility helps him back on his feet. My neighbor mentions her mom died of cancer at age fifty two. "This seems young," she says "now I'm just four years younger than that."

People live longer today, yet disease takes too many early on. We write of the washing machine, and the birds outside. We write of daily routine, each morning we log in a bit more of a story. Early on we aren't aware of where this story leads, much less how it ends.

Still there are people around to keep us on track. They attempt to have us speak in our voice; speak in our voice, echoing theirs. Thus writing is a solitary endeavor. Truly no one can do it for us. This is true for writers, regardless the intentions of people around them, using their voice to tell our story.

Perhaps this is why theirs is still unwritten. It's more than noting the laundry and chirping birds outside. Our writing demands we say something; something in our voice so future readers hear this voice - us. That writing speaks from the page.

I sent a copy of my book to Costco. I hope maybe they will consider another Northwest author for their bookshelves. Listening is the theme of my first book and I hope resonates with Costco shoppers, graduates and future readers. My friend from New York City e-mails he enjoys the book. I include this e-mail along with a short note to Costco.

Today Madeline is on antibiotics. Abby is down to one number on her classroom clocked multiplication tables. She has twelve's to go. She gets math. Yesterday she left behind a stack of past school work. Her writing is good, although she hesitates to read. Still learning is the only lesson, and reading furthers this lesson. Reading is not fun for her.

One day it will be easier if not fun, or at least that is the hope. Mrs. Bush spent much of her adult life urging people to read. It changes lives, a message which resonates from the wife and mother of United States Presidents. Perhaps books placed her there? Or more apt she help lead them because of her reading along the way.

Today I volunteer in Abby's classroom. Later this week there is a luncheon for school volunteers. Thus realistically this is the final week of volunteering with third grade students. Much of the time was spent reading. Occasionally they wrote in their journal. There was also time to test reading speed and multiplication tables.

They have two chances to get their numbers right. Sometimes they do worse the second time around. Being clocked changes the equation, suddenly they have to think quick - literally.

We write at our own pace. Often it's in the same setting where we sit, write and edit. Still we write of other places, people, and times. This morning our friend flies back to London. She has a stopover at JFK and hopes to meet a friend within the five hour layover in New York City.

Last night we had dinner together. The restaurant rolls back their meal prices forty percent on Tuesday. Thus the place is packed, the parking lot full. Now a car makes its way around the loop, people off to the start of a new workday midweek.

I read through *A Sibling Within* deleting words, phrases and sections repeated. We write ongoing yet writing is rewriting. We rewrite what we wrote. Some books say to not only rewrite, instead start all over after the rewrite. Still others say to relive the experience as we edit previous writing.

Suppose after awhile we learn what to keep and what to discard. Keep the watermelon seed, the story seed and weave it throughout. Often we find this much later in our writing exercise. Instead daily we simply fill the page with our every day. The stuff we do day in day out. Awakening kids, school volunteering, the weekly Bible study and those birthdays in between.

We fill in our day with writing and readers relate to this daily rhythm. Still there must be a story seed, in other words our words should say something. My first book says it's called listening. Listen to life and take it from there. This works for all of us, not just writers who listen in daily on their writing.

Madeline is off to sixth grade science out of the classroom. Today she will study marine life, tour the coast aquarium and take a boat ride on the bay. Weather permitting, they will sail onto the open ocean.

Abby slept in and later has a full bowl of Cheerios before leaving with a barrette holding back her bangs. She read yesterday and finished testing for multiplication tables. The number twelve is her final one to beat the two minute stop watch.

Later I help her look up details on swimming. The stroke and kick, one being with arms, the other using our legs. Wyman wrote the first book on swimming in the 1500's.

Another student researches the difference between baking and cooking. One uses dry heat, usually an oven and produces pastries. The other uses oil and often includes meats and vegetables. There are many forms of cooking: broil, sauté, stir fry. Bake too could be thrown in as a form of cooking.

Yesterday was the final day of third grade volunteering. I sat with Marilyn as she told what she thought of my book on listening to life and taking it from there. She too has many stories yet laments she isn't able to word them.

Writing like anything else improves with practice. We see patterns, we get rid of the "get to's" early on. Sooner or later there are less revisions to put on the computer. They don't survive long enough and are edited early on.

Someone is mowing their lawn early this morning. The summer sun is here. Today will be seventy degrees early on. I hope it is boat weather at the coast two hours away. Yesterday I reviewed how many hits there were on my book website. There is also a tally of book sales. The royalties are also listed along with where the book sales occur.

We later went to Red Robin to celebrate. Earlier I'd left third grade students and Mrs. Foster with her jar filled recipe mix for oatmeal cookies. I hope students leave this grade realizing the importance of reading. Learning may be the only lesson, still reading furthers it.

It matters in third grade and later throughout life. We are what we read. It's that simple, or complicated. Futures build by the books we read yesterday, continue today and finish tomorrow.

We write in the early morning as neighbors mow their lawn. Inside I wait for the coffee pot to beep and my morning writing to fill the page. Yesterday I read through notes I took while on vacation in Lake Tahoe.

A spring break road trip. I also wrote on the spring birthday parties. There were several. This story doesn't have a title yet there is a story within those pages. Sometimes it's nearer the third edit before we recognize the words direction.

Today is the final school day before Memorial Day weekend. Perhaps we will take a day trip to the beach. I have a book I want to drop off in Lincoln City. I hope an independent bookstore in downtown Salem will also carry my first book. Getting this one read might open doors for our future books, recording ongoing experience and notes from the past.

Yesterday I sent a letter to Costco. Ideally they have room for one more Northwest author. Exposure moves books. Realistically words move people as well. It's a learning adventure writing, marketing and following along our books once the words are written.

An airplane climbs in the distance on this first day of the Memorial Day weekend. The long weekend started early with the kids off school due to a teacher in service and Melissa taking an extra day off from work. I spent part of yesterday looking for hotels at the beach, flights to the desert or even Hawaii. Many nonstop flights are available at the last minute and for a price. I hoped they would drop fares to fill the airplanes.

I dropped off another book at Jantzen Beach. The copy of my book on listening is no longer on their hallway bookshelf. I placed one there a week ago. I also inserted a bookmark in the hotel's other corridor bookcase. There was a book with the word listen in its title.

My first book speaks on listening; listen to life and take it from there. This works for writing as well, we listen in on our writing and hope future readers enjoy listening along; listening to the distant airplanes and the nearby birds sing in early morning. Today that is the start of Memorial Day weekend.

Maybe we will stay over one night at the beach. They have increased the price of gas, so too for hotel rooms. I also stopped into a Barnes & Noble while at Jantzen Beach. I ask if there is a Wells Fargo bank on the island and as an aside, whether they would carry my book.

Read marketing is often adding in our sales pitch as extra, an "Oh, by the way." Still the salesperson says all books need pass through the main New York City office. I tried, a second time to place my book at Barnes & Noble. I also wrote them earlier in the week.

It takes time to write of the airplanes, birds and those words which are part of our life. Still it takes even longer placing books on store shelves. I placed several bookmarks in books at Goodwill. Those books on listening, finding work or making the most of life.

I figure if they enjoy those types of books, they might also enjoy mine. While there, I meet someone who spent his life in the trucking business.

Dressed in a fedora with suspenders and belt, it isn't the usual outfit. We talk fifteen minutes. He is from Louisiana originally, an orphan with an eighth grade education. I remind him many with more years of schooling don't own their own business.

He says he couldn't see himself on a factory assembly line. Also having a website is no big deal. He has three.

I listen to this colorful character as he searches Goodwill for books. This is my customer, I think to myself. I want them to read my book. Those people are motivated, perhaps forced to be highly motivated by what life deals them.

Earlier he bought a few piano books at one of the major bookstores. He is impatient with his progress. "It took years before I used the piano pedals," I tell him. One day it clicks, we pedal along. So too for those notes atop the keyboard.

As for marketing my book, "Be patient and sell via Craigslist," he tells me as I hand him a copy. Gene wants a signed copy. My first book signing, at Goodwill no less. Maui on Memorial Day weekend would be an early and welcomed fiftieth birthday surprise.

Chapter 21

We are on the "back of the ocean," says Abby. There is no sand visible. Her days at the beach include beachfront, instead we look over several two story homes and the ocean a half mile away.

This morning I write overlooking the Pacific. A wind gust moves the shrubs and berry bushes. Smaller birds fly by along with a lone seagull. Yesterday there were hundreds as we ate lunch at Kyllos overlooking the blues of the Pacific Ocean. Often they are a darker hue or even gray, yesterday they were what most imagine the waters along the Pacific Coast.

The sun shadows play on the north side of our deck. The seagull flies past once again. We will have a late breakfast at a nearby casino. First I'll write up three pages and take a walk along the ocean.

Melissa and the kids sleep in. Abby grunts and shifts in her sleep. Today she may have one less tooth, she was able to put her tongue underneath her baby molar before yesterday ended.

I drop off a copy of my book at Bob's Beach Books. They said months earlier they would carry my book once it is written. Also they plan a book signing for Northwest authors later this summer.

One is planned for August, although it won't be the weekend of the twenty second. I'm happy July's book signing is cancelled as we will be in Vermont for a nephew's wedding that weekend.

Later Melissa and the kids pick up a few groceries at Safeway. I linger in a store selling knick knacks. Mainly gourmet food items, utensils and books.

Racks of books on food. Who knew there were this many written on food alone? "Can I help you find something?" the manager asks. I have written a book and joke it is not for her food bookshelves.

"What is your book about?" she asks. I tell her it is on listening to life. "Oh" she says, "Helen would carry that one." Later we drive over to Salishan to meet Helen. She is not in and we meet Cathy instead.

She greets Madeline, then me. "Helen is off for the Memorial Day weekend," she says "yet I'll call her about your book." She briefly reads the back and the dedication page. "I always read dedications first," says the woman originally from The Bronx.

It's a fun exchange as she recounts parts of her New York as I tell her I too passed through New York, as did my niece now in the Bay Area. Madeline scans the book shelves as we share a few laughs on how life progresses, the people we meet, the people who meet us. People meet us when placing words to the page.

I leave a copy behind along with my telephone number and e-mail address. "I'll buy the copy if Helen doesn't want to carry it," she says. We hug as she carries on about life. I tell her that is the essence of my second book, *A Sibling Within*.

We carry them onward with us, or maybe they take us along. Either way they stand next to us ongoing. "My friend who passed away two years ago is standing right next to me," continues the bookstore saleswoman.

Moving our books off store shelves is a learning adventure. We meet many people along the route marketing our words. Still I prefer having the world listen in on their own lives, rather than restock vending machines with soda or candy bars. I once considered this venture. Now selling books is somewhat similar to restocking vending machines.

I leave Bob's Beach Bookstore with my first sale, seven dollars and thirty five cents cash and stuff it in my pocket. Later emptying my pocket for the day, the dollar bills are there. Somewhere along the route I drop the change. I search the hotel, my clothes, even the car.

It's my first cash receipt for writing. The change is nowhere to be found. Meanwhile Abby places a quarter and dime on the floor beside the bed. I find them upon returning to our hotel room and appreciate her sense of humor.

I wrote my wife had helped write the book which is in each of us. Madeline helped edit, while Abby said parts of it. The store salesperson notes this right away, saying this is the part of books she reads first.

Suppose it says a lot about the author and how those mentioned influence our life. We write for ourselves and thank those who help along the way. Those who help word our books and those who help move our words from store shelves.

"It's a learning adventure," said the woman at Bob's Beach Bookstore. A learning adventure for both of us, meaning me, as writer and Diana, as she learns to run her parent's bookstore. We learn ongoing, running a business and writing books. We learn ongoing influenced by the people we meet. Our books introduce us to even more people, ourselves included.

The sun now brightens up more of the hotel deck railing. Abby groans once again as a bird sings outside. I'll walk the fifty stairs to the beach before everyone awakens; awakens to their day at the beach.

It's low tide. The ocean floor exposes one hundred feet of sea life. Plankton, seaweed and the other stuff Madeline learns about mid week on her trip to the Oregon Coast. They are able to sail on the ocean just beyond Newport Bay. It is a memorable day for her and her sixth grade classmates.

Today I'll return to a Newport bookstore. Gloria, the manager will be in after ten this morning. I hope she takes my book. The Lincoln City library took a copy yesterday. My listen to life book, perhaps now available from Tillamook to Newport, Oregon via the library system.

Books, no different than scattering seeds and hoping some take root. Lincoln City, a tourist stop along the Oregon Coast and one never knows who might pass through. The Iranian hotel manager lamented yesterday beach life is too quiet. There is no place to go for entertainment.

He passes through Germany, New York and California en-route to Oregon. He isn't entertained the Smothers Brothers and Billy Ray Cyrus play at the casino blocks away. Yesterday I left with thirty dollars. A quick seven deals of blackjack and I couldn't lose. I leave after doubling down three times and before my luck runs out. We have lunch at the casino.

Earlier Melissa and the kids shopped the outlet stores. I walk several miles along the beach. It's scenic and windy. I could use a scarf, although most walk in shorts, even more jog through the early morning wind.

We walked through an open house which lines an established neighborhood of condominiums. Then there were the LEED rated green townhouses. The rest of the village is a dozen years away. The economy slows this project in the northwest end of Lincoln City.

These homes are superior to perhaps seventy five percent of American's primary home. Superior in size and craftsmanship. They feel right early on, still only one has water view, the lake, Devils Lake, rather than the Pacific Ocean.

Today I sit and write as the ocean is framed from nine to three. We reserved a partial ocean view yet this view frames the ocean and green lawns of The Inn at Otter Crest.

My favorite restaurant, The Flying Dutchman, is now closed. It juts out onto water on three sides and often there are whales seen in the distance. The Flying Dutchman, a Wagner opera depicting a storm tossed sea within its music.

A quick two hour drive from Portland and a world away. Yesterday I sat on the deck reading. Later I had a blanket and sweatshirt. Still this is not enough to offset the late afternoon cold - wind and cold. This morning it is low tide as birds sing outside amid the calm.

I awoke Madeline earlier so she could check the sea life uncovered by low tide. "Oh yeah," is her groggy response. We are at the beach and the ocean air tires. While at the Lincoln City library, we went online to see if there are hotel rooms available.

Memorial Day weekend and the hotels are full; full and charging holiday rates. Still these condominiums just outside Newport are available. There is a pool yet last night they decide it is too cold to walk back to the room - cold, wet and shivering.

There is also a tram like elevator which glides the slope of this condominium development overlooking the ocean and part of the cliffs to the south. Hawaii without the six hour flight; some days without the Hawaiian sun. Still this morning is calm with blue sky making its way through a light cloud cover.

There is a cold breeze as I leave the sliding patio door ajar. Ideally I sit and read on the glassed in deck although the wind now picks up. Last night gusts kept white caps down below. Today low tide reveals green, vibrant vegetation.

There are eighty stairs should one want a closer look. I walked a similar series of steps yesterday before continuing along the beach. I'm tired and will enjoy my view from the deck this morning. Just me, my writing, coffee and seagulls.

Melissa and the kids sleep in. They walked the outlet mall yesterday. The kids find shoes and new shirts. This shopping area is filled with holiday bargain hunters. There are also sidewalk sales to lure in shoppers. I was at the casino winning.

That's always a plus on our day at the beach. Later I find a few books at Goodwill and drop off a copy of mine. Books like seeds scattered, sooner or later someone will tell someone else. Or at least this is the plan. Even the Iranian hotel manager reviews a copy as we check out. They have a bookcase of stories ready to share with guests. We browse bookshelves making our way along the Oregon Coast this long weekend.

Chapter 22

The laundry whirls clothes clean. We've been away since Friday. Yesterday after a casino lunch, we spent the afternoon walking through recreational vehicles. RV's each more luxurious than the one before. We are told to consider Class A's, the thirty to thirty nine foot models, as we will tire and feel crowded within the smaller and more gas efficient C Class.

We walked a bit of Florence, Oregon after driving just over an hour south from Newport. Parts of the route hug the coast while other highway turns are amid evergreens. We stop at a few rest areas, walking down a meandering path at one. From the path there are three benches to watch Nature's wonder.

Ocean waves crash into ledges, many with blowholes from years of water being forced upon rock. We watch, mesmerized as others climb about. One finds a reading nook just feet away from those jets of water. We hope he scans this area often knowing where to position himself and his reading material.

Earlier I met Gloria. She runs a bookstore in Newport and agrees to carry my first book published. She places it front and center in the Northwest author section. She writes poetry. She completed a book of poems in the mid 1980's yet tires of the selling part of this venture.

We talk as she gives advice on how to move books along. Word of mouth, we agree is what ultimately moves books. She recommends The Chalet restaurant nearby for breakfast. We preferred an ocean view yet the food is excellent.

Abby orders fluffy waffles. They look delicious as she eats them along with some of my pear and strawberries. Madeline has a cheese filled omelet. Melissa has bacon in hers.

They order a second coffee cake once mine is served. I also have a spinach and bacon quiche. The setting is not oceanfront, still it is a memorable breakfast, food alone will stop us should we pass through Newport in the early morning.

I sit on the deck most of the afternoon reading books I found at the Lincoln City Goodwill. One on starting our home business. Continue with our plan and if it is meant to be, one day we will look back despite hurdles along the way; look back and wonder why we hesitated to follow through with our plan.

The other book, a Wade Cook text on keeping more of our money. In other words how to cut out the taxman. This changes through the years depending on how Congress amends tax law.

Before leaving the hotel I walk down eighty steps to view sea life left behind at low tide. People mill around among the now accessible ledges. I later sit poolside and read. There is a six foot glass wall which keeps away wind and allows a view of the ocean nearly one hundred feet below.

It is a wonderful perspective to sit and read of starting our home business and avoiding the taxman. This morning there are seagulls and ocean outside my books. Later I would place one of my own at the bookstore in Newport. Yesterday I was told Gloria would be in at ten am.

She is. Now my book is also there waiting for those passing through the Oregon Coast. Maybe even self employed RV'rs; RV hobbyists among the group.

Chapter 23

The kids are up and at school. Madeline runs early and takes a shower. Abby sleeps until the last minute possible. Both leave their plate of cookies behind; the patriotic red, white and blue plates of sugar cookies.

Midday a friend drops by. We missed the Christmas exchange this year due to weather and life. Our friend battles cancer and celebrates Christmas Memorial Day weekend. Suppose this disease reschedules routes, routines, even holidays. Still she reschedules a cruise once bound for Mexico, now to New England foliage. Swine flu impacts the cruise ship itinerary.

Yesterday my first book was available on Amazon.com. It took a while yet there it is ready to be ordered. Our friend in London calls and says she ordered a copy. She orders from the local Trafford Publishing in England.

She wonders who wrote the back cover synopsis, the words which hope to hook readers. She is surprised I wrote them. Ideally readers enjoy reading along with our words, or maybe consider writing some of their own.

Reading another's story yet filling in our own storyline. No one has the market on story. Each of us has one, our ongoing life, as it is lived each day.

Some days we place our books on store shelves, other times filling in computer surveys of when we would like a book signing. I e-mail August eighth works best. Still I hope to join the Northwest authors at Lincoln City regardless which August weekend is selected.

Having our book show up on Amazon is exciting. Still word of mouth moves books. Another sister e-mailed yesterday. She enjoys my book. She is mentioned in it.

Suppose people enjoy reading of themselves, maybe even their travels long since forgotten: the airport delays and rescheduling, the unexpected sights and stops along the route. The rotations which are story seed to writing.

We write of the everyday and the long Memorial Day weekends. Summer weather is finally here. The kids find a few summer outfits while at the beach. They also get a pair of sandals.

Today is a catch up day, as many take an extra day of vacation. We check the outgoing mail, the bills and run errands. The car needs a change of oil. Saturday the front tire needed air.

The RV show was fun. Still there are too many gadgets which can go wrong. It's all a button away, and works fine early on. Some aren't as mechanical minded, like the woman at the hotel. "Is this the button you turn for bubbles?" she asks.

It's been awhile since she's been in a hot tub. I sit and read beside the pool as she and her friend giggle. Once bubbles start, the giggles start anew. The ocean below with its own share of people looking through tide pools. Madeline learned the names of these sea creatures last week. She even handles a few.

Chapter 24

It's a slow start to a day with two weeks left in this school year. Summer will go by quickly with three trips planned: a week in the Sacramento sun, a week in Vermont for my nephew's wedding, and a weekend in Lincoln City mid August for a book signing.

2008 was a historic year. This was the first time the small publishing houses print more books than the larger publishers; a trend which will most likely continue as more people write. There were over a half million books published last year. Print on demand seems the way to go, with less waste if not roadblocks en-route.

Madeline just came in asking I help button her shirt. She leaves to replace her undershirt. The polka dotted red one shows through her plain top. Abby sleeps in and places an order of cereal.

She probably plans to sleep the summer away. They did for much of last summer vacation. Kids need rest, still exercise is not a bad idea at any age. We write in morning before the pace of life quickens, before school begins.

I've had allergies along with the rest of the family. Perhaps the hotel room was a smoker's room. We leave congested. Several days later and I'm still congested. Maybe it is pollen this time of year.

Another sister e-mails she enjoys my book. It took awhile to read as "busy" is scribbled on her calendar May page. A high school graduation announcement is also in the mail. My niece plans a graduation party along with three friends.

Suppose people combine parties this year. She will attend her mom's alma mater. I wonder how often this happens? Madeline pours cereal from the kitchen. Abby grabs a bite on the way out the door.

She has a project on swimming, Madeline on Latin America. She has her discarded maps on my desk. The printer requires landscape mode to capture all of South and parts of North America.

She colors in countries and waters of the Caribbean in different tints and shades. I tell her many don't have much better than sixth grade knowledge of geography. We learn it in school and quickly forget. Then we have maps at the ready to remind us where El Salvador is located, or if it might be San Salvador.

We know and travel our part of the world. We read about the other parts from afar. Sometimes they are in the news and thus we spend time finding those locations on maps. Mine sits rolled up on the floor. My world map crumbled a few weeks ago and I haven't placed it back on the wall.

Abby eats her breakfast. Midweek, she probably needs to find her library book. Madeline needs sneakers today for physical education. Next year they will be on alternating schedules. One starting an hour earlier than this year.

The other with late start Wednesday sessions. This staggered school schedule will keep the commute interesting. Staggers traffic and juggles our schedules. Interrupts our routine, rhythm to the week. It keeps everyone alert and perhaps that is the idea.

Today the car gets an oil change. I will ask about the Rialto recreational vehicle. Last night looking online there were articles with people attempting to have their Rialtos serviced by Volkswagen. It often ends being serviced by Winnebago.

The weekend RV show had Class A's along with smaller recreational vehicles. We walk through the thirty to thirty nine foot Class A homes on wheels. The salesman says we will soon tire of the smaller space, thus buy Class A. Still with gas prices to consider, a Class C seems more practical.

Today I'll drive across town for an oil change. They often give public transportation vouchers. From there I may go to a nearby shopping center with coffee shops, clothes and computer stores to browse.

The summer heat is here. Yesterday I cleaned up more of the backyard. Plants and tree branches need recycling. Then we went to the Macaroni Grill. From there I walked home and stopped for a Starbucks along the route. Later I walked through a wooded trail with a brook running down below.

At the entrance to the wooded trail is a park. The winding curves of this trail is the front cover to my first book.

Earlier I went to Goodwill. I didn't see my book on their shelves. Someone must have bought it. I later leave with a book on sales. How to get a sale and keep them buying? Sales, a matter of having people buy things. No one likes selling, most everyone enjoys purchasing. Thus, get them to buy.

It's a humor filled read. No doubt the author has used humor to sell product and get out of uncomfortable positions. Whenever one is refused a sale perhaps? Still the book says to venture forward. Don't take it personally. Who knows what is going on in another person's day, week, or even life?

We are to turn the page, march on to the next place of business. Today, while the car gets an oil change, I'll walk through the showroom to see the latest models, gadgets and technological advancements.

Gas mileage a theme for the new administration. Does this mean sport utility vehicles are a thing of the past? Will recreational vehicles come under the higher mileage restrictions as well?

This weekend there is a birthday party for a cousin. She turns six. It's an hour drive down the gorge. There is no off season for the Columbia Gorge scenery. We may go early and have lunch at Hood River.

Watching windsurfers as they cross the Columbia River, the gorge winds push them along. This past weekend someone windsurfed along the ocean. A kite like contraption pulls him across the waves. He makes it look easy, although there are no doubt hours of trial and error. Still he glides across the waves effortless. We watch from a distance as we eat a late lunch along the ocean.

An airplane climbs in the distance the last business day of the month, the last Friday of May. Madeline will wake up, shower and have breakfast. Abby rolls over, eats and is ready minutes later.

School is down to two weeks. Today they have parties planned. Madeline will trade in her violin for a larger size next week. Yesterday the car required new tires; new tires along with that oil change.

I sat three hours overhearing someone pay cash for their new vehicle. They later remark how easy it is to purchase. They leave ecstatic with their new diesel Volkswagen Jetta. Others test drive, debate and leave empty handed.

A bit later a salesperson walks by and offers they have cars for sale. Another gives me a similar spiel. "We have fantastic deals right now," he shares. Still I sit and think how new tires aren't what I had in mind. Even tires need to be replaced on occasion. We will have good tires, reliable tires for our future road trips.

Today I will purchase food and carnival ride tickets for a local fundraiser. It's eighty degrees and I hope this summer sunshine lasts through next weekend of food, rides and community.

I finished reading through the book on sales. It says to have people buy, not so much sell to them. The first thing we sell is ourselves, regardless of product. Sales require a friendly accessible demeanor. We do business with people we like. Friendships account for over fifty percent of sales. Who we know, and more important, the people who know us. As authors placing our name out there is important.

More important is our message which we hope resonates with future readers. Keeping our message consistent gets it noticed. Word of mouth still the best advertisement; one person telling another, one word, one book at a time.

Stories move and the better ones move us enough to share with others. We write for ourselves and hope those who spend time with our words enjoy what we say, or what they say to themselves as they read along.

In an ideal world people compliment and congratulate. In other words, they support and encourage our efforts. Still if people are not satisfied in their personal life, it's difficult to encourage others.

Someone's good fortune isn't always something we embrace. Sales, the book says is an inside job. Like attitude, it must be internal before we express it externally. Those with passion attract us. They live life enthusiastically. Enthusiasm permeates their every day activity.

Enthusiasm gets the job done. Today I search for my pen. It is in the dining room, as I used it last night to keep score for a card game. This morning it writes my three pages; three pages which record our every day, the birthday party for a six year old, the month end reports which show change or at least hint of changes ahead. 2008 was a year of lasting change for many.

Now the end of May we will see if there is a turn in this economy. North Korea continues to threaten. A Central American earthquake leaves hundreds dead. A new day yet troubling for many, their routine is a daily struggle.

Laundry whirls as the kids sleep in. Melissa runs last minute errands and finds a gift for the six year old. Last night her mom called reminding us to bring swimwear. It's hot outside and water games are in store.

I've been fighting allergies since our trip to the beach. Perhaps it was the casino smoke, or maybe one of those hotel rooms was a smoker's room. Realistically, it's the outdoors; the outdoors with everything in bloom.

I checked Expedia yesterday for a week in Sacramento the end of June. Madeline wants to spend her birthday poolside in the California sun. Don't we all?

Later in July we will go to my nephew's wedding. That travel schedule hasn't been confirmed. We wait until last minute for bargains. This works if we can cancel, in other words, if we don't have to attend.

Having flexible plans keep airfares and hotel rates reasonable. Switch to mid week for airfare bargains and hotels for the weekend. We will drive to Sacramento so we can take advantage of the lower hotel weekend rates.

Yesterday I signed up for Chicago's Librarian Book Convention. My book on listening will be on display for the three day July event in Chicago. Ideally several librarians will want my book and order it for their own libraries. One book at a time sells the next.

Still it is people who sell, or more apt buy. The book on sales says this is when things move, once people are in a buying mood. Get them to buy, not so much sell them.

Books move by their message. We are to write a value message. Keeping ours consistent eventually gets it heard. Once it resonates with people, they will pass the word on and sales follow.

The person taking my book fair reservation once managed a Barnes & Noble bookstore. She has an English Literature college degree. She offers the publishing world is in transition.

The small independent presses get their day in the sun. They are no longer shunned and now taken seriously. They compete with the older and often larger publishing houses. Perhaps authors want it this way.

More to the point, readers demand it. They want a level playing field for writers. It's no longer an elite field for the chosen few. Many have written on the notion of guarded writers. Everyone can write as it turns out. Each of our stories as valid and valuable as the next. Still writers take time to write their stories down.

We celebrated a six year old's birthday along the Columbia River. We drive the Mount Hood loop thinking the party is just a bit further. As it works out, it is a lot further. We get to the party as a limbo game is in progress.

Later we find out an aunt fell and broke her hip. Life goes on with travel delays, senior citizen falls and six year old birthday parties. She too fell recently, falling from her bicycle and breaking her wrist.

It's cloudless sky as we eat grilled salmon and birthday cake. Adults mingle as kids run through yard sprinklers.

Chapter 25

I hurry through toast as Madeline altar serves and must leave earlier than usual. "Don't rush me," says Abby. She likes to sleep in and stay up late; that isn't working for her this morning.

Next weekend is the church carnival; a weekend of rides, fun and food. The kids have a bracelet for Saturday, thus they can ride as often as their stomachs allow.

Today I may drive across town to see a friend in a care facility. He too fell weeks ago and has a hard time getting back up. Age and earlier heart trouble slow his pace. Lately it's difficult finding his feet.

We write of travel delays and falls which slow our pace. Ideally we get back up on the bicycle, or the stairs as it were. Sometimes we readjust our footing and carry on. Today another cloudless sky, a change from just weeks ago when the furnace ran.

We took the long route to yesterday's party. I thought it was midway along a loop we drive on occasion. Still it is postcard view of Mt Hood and Mt Adams in the distance, with snow covering their higher slopes.

Snowcapped mountains with eighty degree weather remind we might be in the western United States. Later next month we will drive to Sacramento. Ideally we can drive the Lake Tahoe loop with parts impassable during winter. Reno will have a buffet and a Circus Circus show or three. We will spend the early part of summer break in the California sun.

Madeline wants to be poolside as she turns twelve years old. A dozen years pass quickly. She begins seventh grade in the fall. This year's highlights are a few days of outdoor school and the day on the ocean. They learn of sea life and steer a boat as it gives sixth grade students a tour of Newport Bay and the Pacific.

She learns in the class and outside the classroom. The second half of Abby's last day of school will be in a park. Madeline is done by noon. Abby reminds us to pick her up as usual at three pm.

This year she learns her multiplication tables and the value of reading. Reading improves in third grade and enlightens, entertains ongoing. Reading differentiates lives early and ongoing. This is a lesson I hope third grade students learn this year. It matters to their future, it determines their future. Still they are the ones who must apply themselves.

No one reads for us. Reading a skill improved with practice like anything else we get better the longer we do it. The "doing it" takes us where we need to go says a book on self improvement.

Books on writing say much the same. Begin and continue. Stop when we are done. Still we must begin with the task at hand and some days this is learning to walk once again. Other days, learning new skills, multiplication tables or even reading itself.

A new month begins. Today I will clean up some of the yard. I'll mow and water, a summer routine begins anew this month. A season which doesn't get measurable rain.

The ships came in on Wednesday. These two weeks are full of activity for Portland during the annual Rose Festival. Parades, rides and food entertain residents and visitors alike.

Yesterday while driving across town to see someone in a care facility, I stopped into several estate sales. I leave with two books. One on RVing, the other on Nothing. The Nothing book literally is empty.

Two hundred eighty blank pages wait for our own story; our everyday, recipes, budgets, or travel plans. We literally fill in the pages as we write in what is important to us. Over one hundred fifty thousand copies of the book on nothing have sold. A writer's success story told one blank page at a time - only in America.

Estate sales full of stuff we leave behind. This house is packed, the street parking hard to find. Inside people mill through dishes, linens, clothes and assorted pieces of furniture. I had set out to see an apartment recently refurbished with new carpet, counter tops and paint. A tenant already moved in and the lockbox is no longer available.

I had seen it earlier and wanted to see the refurbished apartment. It's former tenant passed away after living there twenty nine years. Later, I stop in to visit a friend at a care facility. His roommate with Alzheimer's greets me with a hello and a firm hand shake. He is happy for visitors and must be having a good day.

Later I went RVing, reading through a book written by people who are full timers. Thus they travel and live in their recreational vehicle full time. They note there are various sizes from a Class A bus to mere travel trailers. One full of modern convenience, the other allowing the outdoors in, more the camping experience.

There are terms in the RV world, many borrowed from the nautical world. I read through half the book. There are personal stories along with diagrams of their interiors, electrical grid and plumbing lines for water, both potable and gray. They note the connections made while in a campsite, some more basic than others.

The book notes many discount RV's as roughing it. "Give them another look," they say. "They drive easier than most might think." They also have many of the comforts of home.

Some of their furnishings are more upscale than the average home; furnished comfortably, even though in a smaller space. They suggest RV vacations are fifty percent the cost of driving an automobile and staying at hotels. It's seventy five percent cheaper than flying, renting a car and staying at hotels.

Others enjoy them for the spontaneity. Still others for their sense of home, their own bed, shower and living quarters. The setting outside changes depending on where they travel and eventually set up camp. Windows are important as they frame the not so common landscape, seascape or star filled sky above.

We recently went to an RV show. We were in Florence and they had one in the casino parking lot. It is fun and informative walking through the various units. Like the book's authors, Mike one of the RV salesmen, buys the RV lifestyle. They have clubs, membership for people who travel via RV. It's a different mode of transportation and arguably more scenic than a quick flight.

Today there are airplane seats and other parts floating amid the Atlantic. Days ago an Air France flight en route from Brazil to Paris was lost in a storm. Over a year later, I edit these pages after this flight's black boxes were found just days ago.

I read the most dangerous spot in storms is at their top, that's where danger lies. Reading further on recreational vehicles, full timers spend most time in the back of the vehicle. Make sure there are windows there, otherwise while at camp the vehicle's middle windows look out to the vehicles parked alongside them.

There are safer flight paths during storms. There are better seats in RV's. I've been online pricing used RV's. There are many half priced vehicles awaiting new owners. A few vacations and people either buy into this mode of travel or not so much.

Yesterday our car didn't start. It's not good to let a car sit. The AAA guy says ideally cars are driven often. Not good for the battery or vehicle to sit idle for weeks at a time. It slows the day's routine. Later I water and weed the yard. The time of year to mow weekly and prune back on occasion.

Madeline and Abby have their last student council today. Madeline also has a concert. She will play her violin in the orchestra and again on Thursday. Later in the week we will find out if she moves up a size in her violin. There are sizes to violins.

Today is humid, only sixty degrees yet feels much warmer. After the concert I will go to a used office furniture store. I hope they have a wooden office chair. This plastic one eats away at my elbows.

We read of airplanes rerouted due to storms and those which don't make it because of storms. We read of RV's, their passengers and club members. There's a size for everyone books on recreational vehicles have us believe.

Take one for a drive. Roam its interior and imagine living in one. Lie down on the bed. Take a pretend shower. Cook a meal. Relax in the dinette, read, recline - and dream. Soak up the experience and ideally leave the showroom lot with a vehicle; one which takes us places, without leaving the comforts of home.

Some describe them as apartments on wheels. A timeshare salesperson said her unit was a condominium on wheels. On paper this sounds exciting, as a practical matter sometimes it's not realistic or feasible. More apt it's a catalog with prepaid vacation with a middle man helping with the transaction, not unlike tax.

We write of the changing weather, grade school concerts and the books read. Books take us elsewhere, regardless if the story line follows full timers in their RVs. Reading changes the scenery without us leaving our reading nook.

Still some days we upgrade the chair, if not vehicle. I wrote *Twice Found Postcards* on upgrading our view if not sharing special moments with others even years after they leave us and life behind.

Yesterday was the start of tending to the lawn and surrounding shrubs. It's time to upgrade the garden hoses or their nozzles at least. Yesterday water squirted everywhere, and the nozzles no longer turn off.

Some have found the joy of gardening. Others thrive traveling via their recreational vehicles. Still others play music.

Today we will listen as grade school children entertain. They've been practicing awhile. My wife says it is the E string people dread. She knows, having taken violin lessons several years herself.

Music can be noise early on. Writing too needs to be rewritten, edited. Perhaps writing is reading as we fill pages. Still we read of others experience before we purchase similar vehicles;

vehicles which hope to give us a similar experience. Some days the violin takes us along, or this is the hope as sixth grade musicians entertain us.

The sixth grade concert is over. The band played. The symphony later plays in unison. The choir sings a few popular songs. The bleachers are mainly empty. More parents perhaps wait for the later Thursday performance.

Yesterday I walked through several floors of desks. Office desks which are outdated metal. Office desks which are oversized, scratched or marked up. None have my name on them.

Later I walked through several RVs. One has over one hundred ten thousand miles and many more to go, infers the salesperson. He enjoys RVing and finds many retirees, military retirees in particular, do as well. Another lot has the Volkswagen Rialto I want to tour.

The buying decision centers on good gas mileage versus a more accommodating living arrangement. The vans are filled with luxury yet lack space, the open areas are missing. Still others which have more accommodating interior space look like boxes from the outside.

This salesperson doesn't own his own recreational vehicle. Instead he uses a friend's RV or goes along with them. There is selection at every price range. Freedom for some, others see a parking nuisance, if not electrical and plumbing trouble down the road.

The salesperson assures me there are people at campsites waiting for the novice. They wait and help others adapt to the RV lifestyle.

We have dinner at the Olive Garden. Mid meal our neighbors call. They are en-route home from a long weekend at Sun River Resort in Bend. Had they called earlier we would enjoy a meal together sharing their weekend adventures.

Instead we talk of oversized used desks and RVs which are returned early on. Some of them are oversized or otherwise don't fit into the original purchaser's plan.

Later we have a final Bible study for this year. The Acts of the Apostles is discussed, Luke's gospel which continues even today. Jesus' message continues to build church. We are each given gifts, the "grace of the Lord Jesus be with all" is the Bible phrase. What we do with this grace is up to each of us. Ideally we pass it on.

Politics too is in the discussion, this always opens up conversation. Still it's not so much the current political office holder or even the overall economy. If each of our individual lives work, we are in a position to help the next person in line. This eliminates the others, others being a broken political system, a failed economic system, a society which struggles through this recession.

The Acts of the Apostles hope to build community through faith. Even today this is a struggle. There are many distractions, diversions. The grade school concerts mid week, the RV selections, the daily routine which requires our time and energy.

Writing take us away for a few minutes in our day to reflect on life and how we use our God given talents. Are we making life easier for ourselves, meaning helping others along the way. Sharing our grace as it were. We do with our time, talent and resources. We do intentionally on some days, other times we help without realizing it. Even words read years later keep the message alive.

The curbside grass strip is watered as birds sing. I've just opened the house to let some of the cooler morning air in. The past week has been muggy. We water in the early morning and hope grass recovers from the recent heat wave. Abby helped our neighbor water their grass strip last night.

They came home with yearbooks yesterday. A hard cover this year with pages of autographs and grade school greetings. Madeline gave her chewing gum report today. Chewing, one report finds increases our pulse, IQ and memory. It even states gum chewing is good for teeth. Wonder if Madeline succeeds in convincing her audience?

Today she has another violin concert. Melissa and I went on Tuesday. A neighbor will join Melissa for today's concert. Yesterday I sat in a local Radisson hotel reading *A Sibling Within*. Later in the meal I find my credit card is missing. It's always in the same slot in my wallet. Today, it's not there.

I'd left it behind at Olive Garden the night before. They have it ready when I return to pick it up. I have enough cash to cover breakfast, still it is a worry when credit cards aren't where we store them.

"Where can we take a scenic hour long drive?" a couple behind me ask the waiter. The wife discounts Multnomah Falls as she'd seen them years before. Few tourists discount this natural wonder, even if they've seen them many times.

"I hope it brings them to Portland, or Portland to them," I say handing them a copy of my book on finding our place in the sun. They leave in search of a scenic drive. Ideally my book gives them another look at Oregon.

They are elderly, perhaps in their eighties. I mention they are lucky to travel cross country at their age. "The days of traveling to Europe are over," she says. I continue editing, eating my blueberry muffin, bowl of fruit and yogurt. I read for awhile overlooking rose bushes out the window, a lake to my left with coffee at my side.

I am distracted by having to pick up my credit card. We get sidetracked as we write or even eat dinner. A neighbor called mid meal and this added to the situation. I was already running late for Bible study and had to return home for my books before the final Bible study session for the year. We finish up the Acts of the Apostles while enjoying chocolate cake and ice tea.

Today the birds are back singing, before the forecasted thunder storm. The ceiling fan in the family room circulates the colder outside air in an attempt to cool down the house. Otherwise central air conditioning will cool things down. Early June and the summer heat is on. We water in an attempt to keep vegetation green, or at a minimum - alive.

Last night a storm blew in. Looking north the sky was blue with a few scattered clouds. "The forecasted storm didn't materialize," I note to my neighbor as her son plays ball with Abby. Just then my neighbor's husband calls warning of severe weather.

The severe weather the darkening southern sky foreshadows. It is quick. Wind, thunder and lightening. Not unusual for the Midwest perhaps, still Portland doesn't get this weather. It adjust our day's activities and even where we eat. We planned to go to the Spaghetti Factory for dinner, instead we eat at home rather than risk meeting more forecasted hail.

The rain leaves everything greener. The summer heat has turned many blooms. Today I will add fertilizer to help the grass strip along. Our subdivision sends warnings when yards are not green. Even though their own grass strip at our subdivision entrance shows wear and tear.

Madeline had her final violin concert yesterday. At the end, the choir director notes it is the last year for Mr. Anderson. This leaves many in the crowd sad. Retirement exciting for the retiree, yet his students will miss him.

"Did it rain last night? Why is it so dark out there?" Madeline asks from the kitchen. Maybe there's more weather on the way. Abby sleeps in a few more minutes. Yesterday a classmate fell on the playground and leaves him with a chipped tooth. They are down to the last week of school. At month end we will drive to Sacramento for a few days.

My sister e-mails there is a family reunion planned for my mother side of the family. A late notice, and it coincides with our Sacramento trip. We will go back east in July for my nephew's wedding.

Another friend e-mails with details of this weekend's fun festival at the church. She also wonders if I'd published my book. The one she read through months earlier. I e-mail her I am still editing. Yesterday I deleted a few more sentences from the first forty pages. My goal is to eliminate one sentence per page. Now I've got another eighty pages to read through.

It's the fifteenth edit and after awhile we are left with story. We edit until the day we aren't able to edit more. In other words we have phrased our story as best we can. Or so claim the books on writing.

Thus we eliminate sentences and hope to tell our story in the most direct fashion while maintaining flow. Our words, cadence, and story progress at a comfortable pace. We write during the breakfast routine, final week of school, even the unusual early summer electrical storms.

Writing logs in the everyday. It fills our early morning and eventually books, once we've spent time editing the stuff which doesn't further story. We write daily so later we have words in which to eliminate, or better phrase. Abby is now up and prepares for her school day. Her swim report is due today.

This morning Madeline gets measured for her violin. She is still too short or at least her arm length keeps her in the kid size violin. We ate breakfast out and then stop into a used furniture store on the way to the violin shop. A brown swivel round chair catches everyone's attention. Three people can sit in the oversized round chair.

There are also dining room tables, computer desks and assorted other furnishings people tire of, or outgrow. Returning home I fertilize the grass strip beside the sidewalk and cut the now fallen peonies. They are a vibrant raspberry red and later fill the kitchen nook with color.

The kids leave with Melissa to use up more time at the fun festival. There they will find bracelets which let them ride all day. It rained earlier this morning, and I hope by mid afternoon skies clear and the kids get their money's worth in carnival rides. We also prepay for food. Our neighbors will meet us there, for rides, games and community.

My youngest sister e-mails she enjoys reading my first book. "It is cool how they had your name on every other page," she says. She also enjoys reading of familiar people and places.

This is always a bonus if we have been to the places we read about. I'm halfway through reading a book set in Vermont. The storyline follows a doctor's trials; literally a lawsuit and his wife's Alzheimer's.

The setting is familiar along Lake Champlain. The growing old and Alzheimer's storyline becoming more familiar to many families. His wife is down to one word; the word "yes." I read she no longer wants to leave her bed. She is afraid of falling.

We have a friend at a similar stage, although he doesn't have Alzheimer's. We read along, sometimes it's familiar storyline or even family who writes the book. My youngest sister is mentioned in my book. I was there when she was bit by a dog.

Today there is dog residue by our garage door. I hope it is an isolated incident. People take their pets with them, some clean up afterwards, others not so much.

I will join the group at the fun festival. We drive separate cars so we can leave whenever. The rain will dictate the day's events. It's been too hot lately and the rain cools things down.

This morning the telephone rings, although not the one in the bedroom. I had forgotten to plug it in after the electrical storm two days ago. The telephone cord is still unplugged although the answering machine had been reset. This morning it is our friend in London.

She will be in town end of month and has flight details of her trip to Sacramento. She will join us for a few days there. Summertime, a time for a road trip or two. Today it is the church festival. Rain or shine the rides will whirl kids about - kids of all ages.

Birds sing outside. There is a cloud cover again this morning. Yesterday we sat through an afternoon of wind at the church fun festival. The kids enjoyed the slide, snow cones, and bingo. Madeline wins early on. Our neighbor wins playing her first game. Abby has one number left for much of the afternoon and last game, the coverall.

Today there is more fun festival. I will read at home. I'm nearly done a book my sister in law gave me. It's always fun to read of familiar settings, if not familiar people. The author runs the medical clinic where my niece works, thus he signed and gave a copy to my sister in law.

Mid June and the weather has turned colder; cold with showers, not the ideal setting for outdoor activity. The kids sleep in as they played and ran alongside friends for much of yesterday. They were up late and get up later this morning.

The Sunday newspaper is curbside. I ask my daughter Abby to make a cover for this book set in Lake Tahoe and celebrating a surprise birthday in Vermont. "What is Lake Tahoe known for?" she asks. Still I want her insight as to what would attract someone to read of those surprise birthday celebrations. She hands me a page filled with orange balloons floating above a table set with cake. "The wavy lines at the top are the ocean," she says.

The fun festival attendance is down due to the wind and weather. The rides go on and no doubt they will have another carnival to set up down the road. Our neighbor notes many of the workers lack teeth. I suggest they lack routine in their lives. It's a life spent on the road, setting up rides so children can enjoy their day with slides, snow cones and bingo.

It's become an annual ritual for the kids, they look forward to the fun festival. Summer a time away from routine, a time to take a few carnival rides and diet of junk food, if just for one day. We fill up as the wind keeps at our back.

Today I'll stay inside and read. It's a book with small print and big words. The print I notice early on; the big words came later, and too often. Why do people toss in those words? They are as offensive as the bad smile for my friend.

There is a way to tell a story, often it's using words familiar to our audience. We use a similar language so they understand what we relate. Losing an audience early on via big words might not be the easiest way to tell a story. We continue reading, however it colors our experience. The small print is also a challenge.

Still my sister in law wants me to read it. She reads a lot. Something within the story resonates with her. I'm still reading along in an attempt to find that something. So far it's not unlike a cold breeze at our back, or the bad smile. Abby has her report on swimming today. She wants help bringing it in her classroom as she doesn't want the poster board to get wet.

They returned for a second day of bingo. They left yesterday afternoon after losing ten games in a row. I stayed home to finish reading a book begun last month. The thought of wind at my back for hours was deterrent enough.

Later I looked online for places in Maui. One property catches my eye. The realtor, originally from Portland, has spent the last seven years in Maui. The leasehold property is one fifth the market price for an oceanfront condominium. "Don't get too excited," the realtor says early on. The condominium is now purchasing the land, which adds another three hundred thousand dollars to the price.

This makes more sense, although I wonder who these people are with reserves allowing them to purchase half million dollar or more vacation homes. It's the United States and all strata are found within. Some even manage to write books with blank pages, while others use big words, small print or both.

The book I finished reading speaks of our current medical and legal practices; the managing of old age and ongoing lawsuits which clog our legal system. People write what they know, experience and enjoy reading. Writing what we enjoy reading makes writing easier. It flows and ideally readers come along and enjoy the cadence and storyline.

They engage with the story. Early on they want to hear more, not unlike the under priced condominium on Maui. Still it was worth a telephone call.

The Oregon coast asks nearly similar prices and is just over an hour drive. Hawaii of course provides the paradise weather to go along with oceanfront living. Still the website mentions natural disasters, specifically hurricanes on occasion, if not tsunamis.

This wrecks most everyone's day in paradise. We look on line for bargains, the internet allows us to see first hand. We take virtual tours of condominiums in Hawaii. We can also see what twenty million dollars purchases in the Phoenix desert. One property listing is in the twenty seven thousand square foot range. They live large in the Sonoran Desert.

The kids aren't lucky at bingo. Melissa isn't amused when they return empty handed. Madeline won early on the day before, so too for our neighbor. I stayed home and read. Later I took a nap before seeing the places for sale in paradise. Paradise defined differently for each of us, still for many a place overlooking the ocean works. There is movement, the waves keep our interest.

Today Abby tells her classmates the fun in swimming. The origin and exercise benefit of swimming are also mentioned. She has her poster board and note cards ready to go. Now I've got to wake her up. Wake both of them for their last week of school for third and sixth grade.

A car speeds away, our neighbor off to work. The kids sleep in a few more minutes. Madeline has her final violin class with Mr. Anderson before he retires. She has a home made retirement card and Starbucks gift card ready.

He promises they would make music early on. His enthusiasm carries over to the orchestra students. Madeline is sad with the news he retires. Abby gives her report on swimming. She is the last one to give her report. She says the teacher didn't say how she did. She too isn't saying.

I read through *A Sibling Within*. I delete more sentences and find grammatical errors. Melissa later read through the beginning pages. She suggests what voice she would use. "Say it this way. Start here and tell them that," she continues.

She questions my using the word "bucolic." Vermont is often described by this word. We could use pastoral, country, rustic but bucolic comes to mind first. Not so much for my wife, bucolic is too obscure a word; still it characterizes the Green Mountain state for tourists and residents alike.

Birds sing the second day of mid seventy degree weather. The weekend was rain and wind. Today we are back to summer. I will download a few pages of pictures on to cassette disks.

Madeline and I did this last fall yet the cassette disks are empty. We must not have done the second step of writing them to the disks. Now the computer says it's out of storage space.

I hope once the pictures, hundreds of them, are removed from the computer, disk memory won't be an issue. Abby wants to help a neighbor water her yard. This is a first, as usually she jumps in the car and runs errands with mom. Later the neighbor three houses over is outside. So is her grade school aged son. Abby has found a new playmate.

Last week Barnes & Noble wrote they wouldn't carry my book in their nearly eight hundred brick and mortar stores. Space is an issue, also I don't have the editing, sales and marketing cost of the large publishing houses. The rejection letter fills six paragraphs.

I am happy they respond yet the response is politically correct. It isn't so much about my particular book, the story or even because I went the independent print on demand route. Still last night, I find my book listed on their website. This is exciting, if not confusing since they sent a letter saying they wouldn't carry it.

Amazon has my book listed too. They are a popular site for online books sales. I've purchased several books online and Amazon comes to mind first, not unlike the word bucolic to describe Vermont. It must be an older word my wife suggests. Authors have final say on which words to use whether old, obscure or appropriate.

Chapter 26

I am up early. The front lawn strip is watered, the garbage is placed curbside. I tossed and turned throughout the evening. We visited a friend in a care facility after dinner last night. I had several cups of coffee which add to my not falling asleep.

An older sister called mid morning yesterday. She will attend a family reunion planned in the next two weeks. She also spent time finding a place for two extra copies of my book. A local bookstore will carry it. There is paperwork involved before placing it in their front window. Still it is the internet and reliable word of mouth which move books.

Perhaps a few from our hometown will pass and chuckle at the familiar name. Some may even purchase a copy wondering where we've been the past thirty years. Next week makes thirty two years since high school.

My sister wonders if we'll be home for a nephew's wedding. Airfares hold and will wait until last minute for those reservations. Summer and people enjoy seeing Vermont at this time of year. It is bucolic regardless of season.

Yesterday I Googled bucolic Vermont and four pages came up. I stop as no doubt there are even more. Most places have their own vocabulary, phrasing, which captures their essence; even those seen while traveling via Rvs.

Writing is about using the right words at the right time. We have help in this as many express it as merely holding the pen.

We make ourselves available and words take over from there. We stop when a story is told, until then we continue.

Our neighbor waves a hello as I watered earlier. She returns from a morning gym routine. Some get up earlier than others. Yesterday Abby came home with another backpack full of a year's activity, a year's learning. She read through her journal month by month: her favorite class, who she sits next to, her future goals. At the bottom of month end journal entries she draws a self portrait.

She still smiles on the May page. She reads through as Madeline and I listen. She is proud of her progress. Her reading improves after spending third grade with Mrs. Foster. She too packs up as she moves to the recently built elementary school a mile away. Our community grows as evident by the new grade schools. Three now line our neighborhood, replacing the once lone one hundred year old structure.

Progress is good, although our community feels its share of growing pains. Recently the city sent out a survey on whether city hall should process passport applications. A post office might be a more urgent need?

We write of the city newsletters and incoming telephone calls. Sometimes they mention they marketed a few of our books. Some are better at this. My sister persists and now my book is in the store front window. Ideally it doesn't rest there long as I have many more copies to sell. Writers sell their words, experiences, and adventures a book at a time.

Today Madeline has her sixth grade celebration. Parents have free breakfast as kids and teachers mingle; parents too once done eating. Abby will spend part of her last day in third grade at the park. This morning there is drizzle so not sure how this outdoor event will play out.

Yesterday Abby came home with her daily journal covering her school year. She writes of her likes and dislikes. She rates her days throughout the year as some go better than others. "Why was it a horrible day today?" she writes. Other times, "Today was a great day" or even, "I'll sharpen my pencil tomorrow." Still another read, "That was the awful day of my life."

I don't know what to make of it as I read alongside. Actually I want her to expand. Books expand on our good days and the not so good ones. We fill our days with activity, and later write of those activities; sometimes the mundane of writing or mowing lawns. Other times writing how sixth grade graduation ceremonies play out, or follow along with third grade students to a park to celebrate their last day of school.

My sister e-mailed yesterday. The family reunion on my mother's side will include another generation. Some parties happen, others spend time in the planning stage.

We will attend my nephew's wedding next month. Parties always more fun attending than the behind the scenes planning. There are many considerations yet the weather dictates how events unfold, especially those planned outside. Abby is off to the park regardless of the drizzle.

It is Oregon and a little rain doesn't stop the parade, carnival or end of year school activity. Still too often rain falls during the Rose Festival week, annual church carnival and year end school celebrations.

Today we have a full schedule of school activity. Tomorrow the start of summer vacation. Relaxing in Sacramento and Reno is two weeks away. We will sit poolside in the California capital. Later we will eat at casino buffets and maybe watch a show or three while in Reno.

I read through the second half of *A Sibling Within*. I read we edit until there is no more to edit. In other words, we have taken out the stray sentences, those which don't add to story. We are left with story alone. Still to reach this point requires much rewriting. Writing is primarily rewriting.

We continue until we are left with the story we set out telling. Then again, often we begin writing not knowing in advance where the story leads. Thus writing is like all art, it takes on a life of its own. It's in the doing and not so much the end product. Still we hope future readers enjoy our words; they enjoy sixth grade graduation celebrations and third grade park relay races. We hope they are still reading along as our writing and year progress.

They live alongside, not unlike my earlier reading of Abby's journal logging in her third grade routine and not so routine days. The good and "the awful day of my life." Today Madeline is at a slumber party. She left behind sixth grade yesterday, and is awarded a presidential academic notice along with several of her classmates. Later Abby went to the park for the second half of her last day in third grade. She receives the "Most helpful" award.

They play jumping through hula hoops, a row of classmates hold hands as they pass through the hoop without letting go the person next in line. Later they scoop up an egg and pass it along with a spoon. They also attempt to transfer pretzels with a straw in their mouth. We leave before the water balloons start. They enjoy an outside afternoon of fun, pizza and punch.

Madeline had nearly one hundred twenty classmates in sixth grade. The six teachers each give a brief recap of their year.

One notes a classroom of twelve year olds and one forty something is akin to family. She will miss her eight to three pm family. Another mentions putting puzzles together by working from the back, the side which has a family portrait. In other words, what appears front and center, is often because of what happens behind the scenes - family. Family as important as any teacher who may come along.

Another speaks of being new teacher on the block. Her first year and they have a makeshift classroom early on; a portable trailer lodged behind the permanent school building. Another writes a poem for her students, peers and parents gathered to celebrate the milestone of beginning junior high.

Another thanks the administrative staff, volunteers and parents who make learning more accessible. The last, but not least, is Madeline's teacher. She thanks the families, faculty and the students who each applied themselves this school year. Mrs.

Onstott will be one of Madeline's teachers who stand out years later.

It is a good year for her students too, if in fact they applied themselves. Some teachers are more insistent their students apply themselves. In other words learning is something we do for ourselves ongoing. Still some are better facilitators to our learning.

Madeline had her slumber party so Melissa, Abby and I went out for dinner. We eat overlooking the Monarch Hotel pool and clouded over sunset. It begins to drizzle late in the evening.

I read through hundreds of questions Madeline brought home. A series of flash cards test a sixth grade student's knowledge. There are questions on geography, world history, English, math and science. There is also a grab bag category in the Brain Quest series.

It is fun to read through. I miss several and wonder how many I would miss as a sixth grade student. Could I place east to west Turkey, Greece, Italy and Portugal. Can I today?

We learn ongoing; reading, traveling and living a few more decades. We celebrate milestones along the way: the elementary school graduations, and those birthdays in between which introduce new decades.

It's mid morning before sitting to write, there was Sunday service and breakfast first. The food is great although customer service lacks. Perhaps coupons in the daily newspaper keeps them busier than usual this morning. Busy before we walk in, wait - and wait. It is a slow breakfast, turning into a slower morning.

Our schedule off routine. Yesterday I changed pen and now this one has a loose part. It noisily makes its way across the page. I am annoyed after writing the first few words. I hope the package of pens isn't defective.

I work on the opening page of *A Sibling Within*. Those words matter. It is the book's handle. If readers don't grab hold early on they are less apt to stay with us for the remainder of the story.

We write and then spend as much time editing. Placing our words in the proper sequence hoping to use the right ones. We write daily as the outside traffic moves along or kids on roller blades abruptly stop. Sometimes its our pen which speaks to us, its loose part sounds as it moves across the page.

Yesterday a friend wrote. They have a pile of books waiting to read. She is part way through a Bob Barker memoir. Then she will read through my book on listening to life and taking it from there.

It's overcast with light drizzle, not the mid summer weather we expect in Oregon. I have a sweater on as it hasn't warmed up. Midday and even the sun is late in doing what it does best.

Today the kids will clean their rooms. One has been used as a storage space for weeks now. Madeline has an early birthday party with classmates coming up and this motivates her to clean; or motivates mom to oversee the task. Clearly some of it is for the recycle bin at this point. There are only so many school projects we can store. I know, I recently went through an attic of treasures.

Abby's backpack contents still cover the living room floor. She cleaned out her desk filling two backpacks. Now their contents sit on the house floor. She too will have to decide which notebooks, journals and projects to keep.

I went home last month to celebrate my oldest brother's sixtieth birthday. I brought back a bag full of mementos: letters while in the army, some high school and college reports. They now sit in the garage where they landed. Eventually, we sort through our stuff.

Often they manage to find their way into our writing. We mention this biology notebook we share with our daughters. The teacher had graded our ongoing science scrapbook. Some notebooks are more memorable than others. It takes us a year to fill with notes, sketches and experiments.

Still we purge from time to time not unlike writing which demands we edit ongoing. We take away and later are left with story only. The parts others enjoy reading, long after the opening page handle.

This morning I'll water the curbside lawn strip. It's been awhile since lush grass stood. Our neighbor's friends trampled it throughout the winter and early spring, now grass has a rough time springing back to life.

I'll water and hope for the best. Two weeks ago I fed it fertilizer mixed with weed killer. There were a few days of rain afterwards and still the grass struggles. The kids sleep in the first week of summer vacation. I was up late watching a movie on finding work in San Francisco. Finding reward in life, pursuing happiness as it's elusive for many.

We expect green curb lawn strips. Children to wake up early and fill their summer vacation with activity other than sleep. To find work which fulfills and leads to happiness. Writing is an ongoing process which fills our every day. Later we have people help edit. They find grammatical errors, repetitions, and the erroneous time sequences. Editors are accountants with red pens.

Yesterday my wife mentions I already noted the election results. She thinks I can't mention politics later in my story. I feel different, and leave the political insight in. It goes along with my story, it parallels life at that time.

Events reveal themselves ongoing, not unlike writing which says something as we write further. More apt, after hours of editing we are left with words we like and readers who come along to read our stories.

Today I'll water the grass and perhaps recycle a few things. The kids have a bag ready from cleaning their rooms two days ago. There is plenty in the garage to sort through, now summer is here. We could drop off a few carloads.

This is the goal for the next two weeks before leaving on vacation to Sacramento. Ideally the grass will have sprung back to life. We water and hope for the best.

Today is overcast. Much of the weekend was also cooler weather for mid June. I have a sweater on as I water the yard. Later we may go to a store which sells office furniture. It's time to replace my makeshift desk. They have some nearly sixty percent off.

The kids sleep in. I'll let them rest until after the outside watering is done. They were up late reading, they read as their i-Pods played. I wonder how they manage to concentrate.

Abby says she is already on page one hundred fifteen. I don't ask which page she started on. We often write by starting in the middle of story. Other times by our morning routine, the one which includes watering lawn strips not revived from a winter of snow, ice, and maybe trampled from visiting neighbors and friends.

Chapter 27

This morning The World is docked downtown Portland. A floating thirty two story condominium residence. People who call the world home as they sail around it ongoing. It's one way to travel, an experience reserved for this segment with deep pockets.

Yesterday was the first week of summer vacation. We recycled our cans and bottles, and then went in search of a home office desk. The one advertised is too small, thus the equally low price. Later we walk through Ikea.

They have desks and most any other furniture or household item one might want. We settle in for lunch of meatballs, mashed potatoes and cranberry sauce. For dessert we try apple strudel and return for the chocolate cake, which goes better with my coffee.

Then we browse Marshall's, Ross Dress for Less, Staples and Best Buy. Abby finds a duffel bag for weekend trips. I find a couple pillows. We also leave with a shirt from Ross Dress for Less and check out home office furniture at Staples. They have a desk which has potential.

The floor model is marked down and equally marked up. I may order this particular desk model online. At Best Buy we look at computers. The kids have fun stretching their faces in virtual contortions. The Apple computer lets them with its built in camera feature.

Madeline wants one. I too want a replacement computer for our desk top which is temperamental at best. Today will be near eighty degrees. The cloud cover left early on yesterday as summer heat returns.

We walk the new Cascade Station shopping area as airplanes fly overhead. They land within minutes. The airport literally one more stop down the light rail track.

The kids sleep in although today they will clean more of Madeline's room. Maybe we will drive downtown to see the floating residence, all thirty two floors. Portland on the world map, or at least a stopover for those who spend their life cruising the world. I'd seen this living arrangement advertised several years ago. If one has to ask price, they are priced out of this floating real estate market.

The ship is registered in the Bahamas and residents represent a slice of the entire world. I wonder the Portland connection. Did they just float up the coast in town from San Francisco? Or is there someone local onboard?

How exciting for them to drop by their primary residence. Anything is possible today if funds are available. Yesterday we were sold wireless web surfing as we walked through aisles of computers. No doubt we are headed toward a wireless world.

It gets easier each day to travel whether via recreational vehicle or the luxury of a world cruise ship, one which takes personal communication along. Technology changing, adapting as we change living arrangements. Perhaps we change due to the ongoing developments in technology. A year later I edit these pages after spending last week joining that wireless world.

Today is a catch up day. Madeline will clean her room. The one she promised to clean last Sunday; one promised clean for a month now. Today Abby and I will help her sort; some of it will be thrown out, some for Goodwill, and the rest will make it to clothes hangers in her bedroom closet.

Yesterday we dropped by The World. We had breakfast at a local restaurant which sells organic bakery goods. Later we drove downtown in search of the world. The World being the cruise ship with the Florida mailing address. The ship and its one hundred fifty six residents floats around the world. These people are fortunate to have water view ongoing.

We walk along Tom McCall park which borders the Willamette River. We walk along the seven hundred foot ship. We count as we pace along.

Many locals have cameras at the ready. I have a copy of my book. I visit with a couple who leave ship for the sights of Portland. They will place my book in the ship's library. Now my book takes another route out of Portland. We do what we can to market stories.

Later we place another copy at a Jantzen Beach hotel. While there we walk a bit of the Columbia River boardwalk and see an older Lincoln Continental, teal with white top. I tell the kids this car is over forty five years old, older than some people they know - people they know well.

Madeline took pictures of The World. She also takes several photographs at the Jantzen Beach hotel parking lot with cars from Canada and various states: Missouri, New Mexico, California and Washington among the local Oregon license plates. I wonder which one will take my book further.

I leave a copy on the hotel bookshelf. The one which invites guests to exchange books. We later walk through several stores, looking for electronics, clothes and books.

At the Barnes & Noble store, Abby is reminded computer terminals are for employees only. Still we leave with my book on the computer search screen. "We have seven hundred ninety nine Barnes & Noble stores left," I joke leaving the bookstore.

Who knows who's onboard the world? Realistically the world is represented among the residents and their guests on Residen Sea, The World.

My book is categorized as biography. The challenge is writing a book not easily categorized. Thus it is also placed within the self help, travel and maybe business sections. My first book covers those areas. My wife wishes it was more specific. "Tell one story only," she suggests.

Others enjoy the change in pace, setting, if not storyline. Thus we write for ourselves first. We write what we enjoy reading. I hope those onboard The World enjoy the slice of life, the portrait of Portland I tuck within. I hope they leave this temporary dock with a better appreciation of the Rose City and maybe one of its residents.

The kids rooms are cleaner this morning. My den too has less stacks of paper. Midway through cleaning, my college roommate calls. He lives in Florida and we connect at least yearly via the Christmas letter.

We talk a bit of current life. What goes on in our day to day? I mention we are in the midst of cleaning house. The kids are midweek in their first week of summer vacation. He mentions his trip to Paris earlier this spring.

He wonders if I am still a stay at home dad. I mention I wrote a book. While he is happy to hear of my new venture, he wonders why I didn't tell him? He also wonders if he is mentioned in my book. He is, in the second one.

And this third one, as his name is printed beside my stack of pages as reminder to consider what he would hear reading this story.

We write of our everyday and those telephone calls which come in once a year. We might e-mail more often. There are cycles to life and this goes for relationships as well. I mention him in my book *A Sibling Within*. I have just told him about the death of a Tenderloin hotel resident.

People pass on. When they are mid nineties we grow to expect this. When they pass on as children, it gives us something to write about. It is less expected at that age. I edit this a year later, weeks after finding out my sophomore college roommate passed away. I often share the antics of Andy with my kids. They laugh today. I laughed back then.

Madeline has a slumber party planned Friday. They have a few bags ready to recycle: toys, shoes and clothing they outgrew. They have one too many school projects around the house. We will prune them back as well. When it all becomes a keeper, none of it is worth keeping.

A neighbor drives off to their work week. My pen still noisily makes its way across the page. This pen is defective yet I'll continue until the ink dries. I'll listen through a few more pages as it works out.

Today we fill the car with recyclables. There are books, a Christmas tree and clothing which will find new life at Goodwill. Someone else will enjoy reading those stories, have a new Christmas tree or even a new outfit.

Abby answers the telephone when my senior year college roommate calls. Later she wonders who is on the line. I hope she too is fortunate to have a college roommate, one who travels life alongside everyday going forward. Regardless how often we connect, there is a relationship, one started over twenty five years ago.

We celebrate milestones. We share our lives with each other. We include them in books. They know our book's opening line as it works out.

"Each of us has one, I find three without searching my room." I'd meant a calendar back then. Today it's about books as I write more of mine. Still some days it's about friends, those found decades ago in college and now within our own books.

Today the cruise ship floating home to a lucky group of one hundred fifty leaves Portland for Astoria, the Washington state San Juan Islands and eventually the world. Thus its name The World.

I once lived on Main Street, New York, New York. I thought this was a clever address. Still having a ship The World as home is probably as good as it gets. The world literally floats by our front door, side deck and even family rooms.

Today it rains. It's been an off few seasons. Winter record snow. Spring nonexistent. Summer having trouble heating up. Mid June and we wait for a semblance of summer.

Rain will not stop the community garage sale planned yearly for this weekend. We participated one year and lack customers as our own neighbors sit in their garages full of stuff waiting for buyers to come along.

The kids clean more of their rooms and now carpet is visible. There are a few more bags for Goodwill, as I place them in the car trunk. Our neighbors wave from across the street. I later join them.

They mention a friend and his mom are onboard The World touring residences for sale. I am envious. Our neighbors laugh at the thought my book will sail away with The World. I'd asked a passenger to place a copy in their onboard library.

"It's called listening," is the book's last line, and a notion I hope future readers appreciate. Life opens for each of us once we listen: to others, ourselves, even our writing. Future readers read along with what we once experienced, heard and write down.

We write of visiting cruise ships, neighborhood garage sales and the neighbors themselves. Melissa will come home early from work as she wants to walk through a few garage sales. There are over one hundred seventy listed as participating in this year's neighborhood sale.

We have our own garage full which slowly empties as we drop things off at Goodwill. An airplane climbs in the distance. Yesterday a pilot died mid flight from Belgium to Newark, New Jersey. There are doctors onboard, yet the pilot has a fatal heart attack. There are several pilots onboard thus the flight continues as planned, less the senior pilot.

Today The World sails down river to the Pacific Ocean. They are off to see more world. Some perhaps have already been around the world once, while others marvel at the ship's size. Some lucky ones tour the inside. Still others enjoy a front row seat from their living rooms, home aboard the ship, The World.

There is little sun this morning. There was little sleep last night as the slumber party ended at ten pm. The slumber party ended at two am. The party went to sleep at three thirty am. Now the group of seventh grade students lingers in the family room. Madeline fits in an early party before we celebrate her twelfth birthday in Sacramento.

They eat pizza, cake and play games. I leave with a load for Goodwill and return a shirt I recently purchased at Ross Dress for Less. "It didn't work for you?" the clerk asks. Earlier I had a carload of clothes which no longer worked. Most of it outgrown, others the kids received as gifts, isn't their style or even "chokes" them.

Walking through the Happy Valley annual garage sales, I find a book on various card games. Another book suggests something different to do with each of the three hundred sixty five days of the year.

Later I find one on the New Testament. It is written in prose and makes easier reading without numbered passages. In theory it also translates the New Testament, the second part of the Bible for us.

There is also another book on standing up for ourselves, standing up on the inside. In essence confidence moves us further along. The worldwide lecturer speaks of her struggles along the route.

While the birthday celebrations continue, I leave to run errands. I later find two more books. One on the internet; commerce on the internet and how this changes each day, affecting each of our futures.

We are either online or fall behind. While traffic is desirable, it's quality of those website hits which matter. In other words repeat customers keep business afloat, even the online businesses. Perhaps businesses of the future will focus less on local brick and mortar, and more on global reach.

I also find a book on music; music a design for listening. We hear well enough. Listening, on the other hand, takes effort and concentration. Even music is enhanced once we listen in layers if you will. We note particular parts yet hear the entire musical piece right alongside the segment we concentrate and focus on.

The slumber party slowly awakens. Several will take naps later today. It's exciting as kids to stay up a bit later than usual. Still it's not a good habit as kids or even as adults. Sleep, exercise and a balanced diet keep most of us healthy and in shape.

The summer sun lacks again this morning. Ideally the several days of rain will renew lawns and sidewalk strips. Ours has been trampled and struggles to revive. "Water," said a landscaper years ago, "water alone brings back most lawns." Today the mid summer rain will do the watering.

Just now Melissa opens my den door and says she'll be right back. She is off to get a dozen donuts, maybe more. Ideally Madeline's classmates will be long gone once the sugar kicks in.

Chapter 28

The blinds are open. There are patches of blue sky, still it is a cold June morning. Today is Fathers Day. We will have breakfast at home: eggs, bacon, juice and coffee. We might drive to the coast later, visit a friend in a care facility, or stay home and read. Today is open, just as the date opens summer for us all. The first day of summer yet sweaters are welcomed.

I overhear them counting eggs as they drop into the frying pan. Today we make time for a huge breakfast. There are breads from Costco along with day old donuts. Just now they stir in milk.

Yesterday we watched as they televised a cake competition. The goal is to make a birthday cake for someone. One cake doesn't make the final cut, instead a fire extinguisher saves the day, although not the cake. Some are decorative and ornate, while others are judged a shade too dull.

A sport utility vehicle drives along the loop. They are perhaps in search of a garage sale. Today the intermittent sun may help sales. Friday and Saturday were rain and cold, not ideal conditions for garage sales.

The cooking continues two rooms away. We will have an omelet and coffee. "Whatever you want," Madeline says. We also have left over pineapple from Costco.

Two days ago we used a plastic contraption which slices pineapple. Around the pineapple it twists, leaving slice and core separate. Still it is always fresher if not more work spending time slicing the pineapple ourselves. We thought it was from Hawaii, instead the pineapple is from Honduras.

Abby joins in the kitchen conversation. They work on breakfast as the timer goes off. Are they using the oven or just the timer to help with the meal?

Now bacon permeates the house. We will have a full breakfast this Father's Day. We will eat at home and then take the day as it unfolds.

Maybe a Sunday drive is in the works. First having sun break through the clouds would help set the tone, overcast skies keep many indoors. Just now the furnace kicks on. Strange weather for the furnace to run. We run it through the other seasons and hope it's not needed during summer.

Still this morning the furnace runs. We will eat breakfast and take the day at a leisurely pace. Already my morning writing is delayed two hours.

Madeline stops in my den asking measurements for making coffee. She insists it's for future reference. Still this too will permeate the house in minutes. Later coffee's on. Thus the breakfast is ready, to serve and enjoy on this Father's Day.

Chapter 29

The lasagna is now eaten. Tomorrow we will eat another serving of this Father's Day lasagna. Madeline made the salad as Abby helped mix ingredients for lasagna.

Later in my den I read through some books I found at the community garage sale. I write in a few notes in my journal. Notes and information I might read once again or weave those ideas in my own writing.

I read through a section on doing versus being. I too wrote an entire chapter on this notion. We are much more than what we do day to day, our being matters. Once we are gone, this is the part which remains. We are no longer available to do, yet being remains, our soul lives on and survives us.

Last night an e-mail came in from one of my sisters. My youngest sister has lost her mother in law to cancer. I hope my sister connects to this idea of being, more so now her mother in law is no longer around to lend a helping hand.

Some are lucky enough to enjoy our mother in law's company. When they leave it is not a good day, or week. Still if they impact our life, they live on. I wrote about this idea in my book *A Sibling Within*. Thirty five years later they still influence life, they write our words alongside with us.

I read about being and doing. Another book previews the changes ahead due to the world wide web. It is a way to meet people. It allows a broad reach, a global connection. The most successful products reach a broad market yet retain a personal touch. Thus the internet is a personalized medium.

Think of it as a funnel. Television, radio and even newspaper reach the masses and thus are the top part of the funnel, wide and far reaching. The internet has a more targeted audience thus it is the bottom of the funnel. The better websites keep customers coming back. They are likely buyers and a good website sells to those niche customers.

Internet changing the way we sell products and the marketing behind purchasing decisions. Even malls adapt to the changing world of commerce. The internet takes some of their merchandise sales. Thus malls adapt by adding more food and entertainment to the mix. Less merchandise and more eateries with places to linger and spend.

Our mall recently upgraded its facilities. True enough they add restaurants and theatre seats. Internet changing our world, even the one offline and just around the corner.

The kids pack some of their clothes for our upcoming trip to Sacramento. Packing a week early, they are excited. Today with cold overcast skies, the California pool is more enticing. I read further through some of my garage sale finds. Now I know what people in their gated communities read.

They read of the internet, various card games and God; God and his place in our lives. Books, the things we tell strangers, are filled with everyday and those days that aren't. Those days which change us, and leave us a changed person. Sometimes it's through meeting someone new, leaving others behind or maybe even hearing from someone through books they write.

Last night, I watched a program which predicted how life would look one day after people, one week after people, the world years after people. They had Manhattan flooding, crumbling then springing back to life with water, vegetation and nature taking over. Vines grow alongside the few remaining skyscrapers.

The Roosevelt Island tram cable would eventually fray and drop the tram into the East River. I watch seeing sights once part of my everyday. I took the tram daily to my job in lower Manhattan.

They also show how the dozen or so breweries in St Louis would manage without people to oversee the brewing process. The vats would eventually blow their top. The explosion would damage nearby buildings, or at a minimum move many nearby roofs.

The St Louis Arch would last for years. Still one day the top piece would fall, causing a cascading effect. The two remaining pieces would collapse onto each other without linchpin which holds them together.

The train ride up through the arch's interior and accompanying views atop would be history. We took this tour in the fall of 1993. We drove through the Midwest, a place marked by its recent flood as we drove from Texas to the west coast, stopping in Iowa en-route.

Iowa had snow and later crossing into Washington state rain began to fall. Today the sun keeps it in the low eighty degrees. I'll mow the lawn and hope to get a new key for the Toyota. The first replacement key was defective. We leave for Sacramento in a few days and handy to have duplicate keys along for the ride.

I'll also water the lawn strip along the sidewalk. It still has patches of brown even after the past few days of rain. Not the best of soil to grow things apparently. Even Manhattan allows vegetation with its abundance of water and sun.

It was fun to see how the world would look without humans around. The buildings would leak ongoing. No one would change light bulbs. One light in Times Square would continue until the bulb burns out. They use solar and wind power to generate electricity. Still no one would be available to change this light bulb.

Today Melissa gets a replacement battery for the Toyota duplicate key. Early on the battery went dead. So too for the kitchen telephone. Yesterday we found a twenty dollar replacement battery, almost the price of a new telephone itself.

There were Sedgeways at the electronics store. At five thousand dollars each, perhaps there won't be one in every American garage. There are more reasonably priced bicycles says the salesperson.

He moved from the Phoenix area and notes many college faculty members use Sedgeways in the Arizona sun. I tell him Phoenix has the third highest concentration of millionaires. He didn't know this.

Later another salesperson helps us as we browse computers. "Go for a desktop if you don't need mobility, otherwise you pay more for a smaller unit," he says. "The Apple brand last longer, it outlives the competition," continues this salesperson. He shares his website and a book read awhile back. I ask about the Mac's ability to create web pages.

I-Web, create your own online space. Still it requires a web host. Their prices have come down as more people have personal websites, a web page. The store salesperson has one on photographs. He is a photographer, having traveled distances, even abroad to take pictures. He says creating a website and having someone host it is not complicated.

For those who struggle with physical cables on computers, it's sometimes difficult to understand routers, web hosting, and other jargon unique to the digital world. Still we learn ongoing. Editing a year later, I realize we now have our own family room router.

Yesterday I saw there was free delivery to India. A website has my book listed and the delivery is free, to India no less. Slowly we realize the reach of the internet. I'm midway through reading a book on how the world wide web will change life going forward.

There are now three million books in print at any one time. Recently Amazon.com had two point five million of them available. A giant bookstore is only able to warehouse one hundred seventy five thousand books. The internet changes marketing, regardless what we sell, or hope others purchase.

Being online makes the difference. Without an online presence, a web page, businesses fall behind. Selling information, which books are primarily in the business of doing, moves inventory. Access is not limited once products are online, available to the world, sometimes postage free.

The kids sleep in. Later we will go out to breakfast and then stop for grass seed. I will reseed the front lawn strip as it's proving difficult reviving after the past year of record snow and ice. Shrubs and a few trees will need replacing too, once we return from summer vacation.

The Sacramento week is booked. I'm still waiting for better airfares before making reservations for a nephew's midsummer wedding in Vermont. This is a month away, however not free delivery.

The garbage is curbside, the start of a typical Thursday. The kids sleep in as Melissa leaves for work. Today she is on a late schedule. I reseed the lawn strip along the front sidewalk. I hope this turns the area green. A neighbor rolls their week's discards to the end of their driveway. It's early morning and not much else moves about, inside or out.

Our neighbors roll a second container to the curb. Thursday a day to throw out debris and recycle more. I came home yesterday with a brochure on sustainable living. There is also a pamphlet on an upcoming home recovery seminar.

Lots of the country struggles. Our once enviable neighborhood now partners realtors with city officials in recovering homes, our community. We walk through Home Depot after a breakfast in Gresham; a new breakfast spot the owner says has been open nine months.

Later I point out the newer hospital to the kids. They were born there nine and eleven years ago. Next week it will be twelve years for Madeline.

Next week we will celebrate poolside in Sacramento. We will also drive to Reno for a day. Central California as good as any place to sit, lounge and write in the sun.

The kids are already packed. Ideally they have fun family vacation memories. Still other trips we schedule months in advance, planning them is part of the excitement.

I e-mail Diana at the Lincoln City bookstore. She asks we reserve a space for the mid August book signing. This is a first and will be a learning adventure.

We are to step up and out is how a book phrased it. Be bold and venture forward trusting the process. The author wrote of living our best life.

She infers we are to place ourselves within, place God there too. Listen for his guidance and direction. Ask and believe he hears us. Have faith things work out as they should.

Sometimes this is not on our timetable or planning schedule. Still know this all works out for the best, even if we question along the way. I'd found this book at last weekend's community garage sale. At least this household behind the neighborhood gated community read of him.

They had a shelf of religious books. I leave with two and now will continue reading the New Testament, written in prose. Thus it's easier reading, in theory at least. Someone wrote in the hope of translating the New Testament for us.

Our writing translates experience. We in essence sign our writing. Each of us tells it differently, although we may share a similar destination or story theme. We write in our own voice hoping others not only hear us, they hear themselves. Or open them to hearing the voice beyond, silence which is his.

Chapter 30

Laundry whirls. Today is full of activity and last minute details before leaving on vacation. We will stop at the bank on the way to the airport to pick up a friend. She flew in overnight from Amsterdam. One of the more direct flights from her home in London to Portland.

Michael Jackson has fifty concerts scheduled in London, beginning next month. He died yesterday of cardiac arrest. Some argue he was the most recognizable face on the planet. Others wonder if his legal matters will ever get sorted. Still others suggest yesterday was a collective, "Where were you?"

Many remember where we were when Elvis, John Lennon, Bing Crosby and even Anna Nicole passed away. I had just finished army basic training when news spread of Elvis' death in August 1977. John Lennon was shot while I served in Korea in the early 1980's. For Bing, I was en-route to California for the first time. Anna Nicole, I'd have to think about this one.

Yesterday I called my wife to chit chat, adding Farrah Fawcett had died. She fills me in with late breaking news; news which would clog newsrooms and keep them busy for weeks. Those near fifty hope we don't pass on at this otherwise midlife milepost. Still depending on our daily routine, some age faster than others. Death takes each of us, whether via the slow disease route, or an abrupt heart attack.

The laundry fills with water. I'll finish a few loads before the trip to the airport. I'll water the yard and look over bills before we head for California sun and add more expense. The kids sleep in.

Later they will finish last minute packing as their suitcases have been packed for days. Madeline looks forward to her poolside birthday celebration. Abby too looks forward to days spent swimming. They will shop at a local outlet mall and see a few shows at Reno's Circus Circus casino.

It's a cool morning. Yesterday the sun finally broke through a heavy cloud cover. Today clouds keep the sun hidden, blanketed away. Several birds sing outside.

Last night the media was in overdrive. This morning the world takes in the events of yesterday. The self proclaimed king of pop is dead. So too for Farrah Fawcett, a girl from Corpus Christi whose image also circulates the globe.

She was beauty at it best. Those close to her know she was more than mere physical attractiveness. Suppose the most attractive are more than symmetrical, much more than being balanced in facial features. They brim with vitality and we notice.

Others spend a large part of life augmenting or physically changing their appearance. Sometimes it works, other times leaving them with fragile features. Some would suggest the medical community has a role in this. They need to say no somewhere along the process. One more procedure is out of the question.

Yesterday will be remembered by a collective, "Where were you?" Regardless of age, part of pop culture left yesterday yet lives through their work, posters, music and being.

Today we drive to Sacramento. The kids packed the car last night. This morning they are ready to go as they roll out of bed. "A friend eats tobacco," Abby mentions. Later she thinks it might be "Tabasco".

We went to the airport to pick up our friend yesterday. We walked the skywalk from parking garage to the terminal. Later I drive the car around to pick them up as they look for our parking space. They had returned on the parallel skywalk and thus look in the wrong row of cars.

I had gone ahead to use the self pay kiosk to pay for parking. Earlier there was no drinking water available with our Subway sandwich purchases. Thus I wanted to leave the airport without paying an additional hour's fee.

We drive home and await further news of Michael Jackson. His passing carries the news headline. Still mid afternoon a day later and the details are sketchy. The preliminary autopsy reveals no external body trauma.

Rumors are rampant as are comparisons to Elvis and others who recently passed away early in middle age or before. Today we will drive to the California capital and enjoy a few days of sunshine. The house is locked and prepared for us to be gone awhile.

The kids will swim. Melissa will enjoy the lack of work routine. I too will enjoy the summer sun late in finding Portland. Tonight they forecast high thirty degree weather; strange weather for mid summer.

Reading more of my community garage sale finds, Dr Dyer's book on the Tao says to follow nature. Be like water, the ocean and serve. Low ground collect the rivers, streams as they return home.

He describes Maui as he writes. We experience the sea breezes and see the rainbow which stretches from his home's window to the surrounding island of Lanai. He places us there. So too for Lau Tzu who wrote twenty five hundred years ago. His message still relevant today. Dr Dyer translating those passages for us.

I read further, stopping to reflect on his message. It's not a book quickly read. I jot down a few notes as I read. Recall is better if we take the time to write things down. We in essence write them on our minds via writing them down on paper.

We jot down ideas and later implement them in our lives or word them in our writing. We apply someone else's translation and in the process make the words our own. We use them within our everyday, even those days we pack for Sacramento.

Chapter 31

Mid morning I sit poolside. Sacramento is already baking. I have one side of the cabana screened off. Still it's sweat weather poolside as kids dare each other to dive.

Madeline and Abby have been swimming since breakfast. They too have found a spot in the shade. Earlier we had breakfast in the hotel lobby. Then I read the local Sunday newspaper.

The Sacramento Bee has stories on Farrah, Michael and the record heat. Precautions to take due to the heat while other columns deal with finance, life and death. One notes how to find a thousand dollars alongside and within our everyday.

Another laments they were given gift bags at a recent funeral. Among other items are a bit of the departed's ashes. "Oh dear," begins the columnist's response. Not a good idea at a funeral, amid the summer heat wave, or any other time for that matter.

Writing fills the early morning. Writers write ongoing: beside pool splashes, the kid summons or adult responses they can't help their children find pool items. They can fetch them themselves as it works out. Words and everyday experiences find their way into our ongoing morning writing venture.

Last night we found the local Spaghetti Factory. They were busy yet sat us upon entering the family restaurant. There are tables of children beside us. This restaurant began in our hometown Portland in 1969.

The pool is once again full. There are three languages. Each group swim, splash and encourage their family members.

It's hot enough to dilute my pen ink. This morning it doesn't sound as it writes. Rather the ink is thinned by heat and thus glides along the page. We write first thing in the morning, other times closer to midday. Still other times we make mental notes as we drive along.

Yesterday Abby noted this is not the place for motorcycles as we drove five lanes of freeway. The drivers suddenly more aggressive as they make their way east. There weren't many clouds along the route. The Redding, Red Bluff area has an earthquake hours before we pass through. We looked forward to leisure time poolside and instead the pool is full.

Today the hotel pool keeps everyone cool. The breakfast crowd now congregates poolside. The cabanas are full. Others are in full sun, baking early in cloudless central California.

Abby gets her i-Pod as I return to the room for my pad of paper for today's three pages of morning writing. Later I'll review pages written on spring break in Lake Tahoe and a sixtieth surprise birthday party in Vermont.

I've been asked to write on family. Having a dozen siblings there are plenty of storylines. Losing a five year old sister wrote *A Sibling Within*. A book on the birthday party for my oldest brother has not been titled.

It's still being written yet will require many revisions along with that title. We write in early morning and then spend days even months finding the story within. Writing is a series of rewrites, even those initially written poolside in the Sacramento heat. Poolside we log in more of our life and the lives around us.

The sun bright, sky a cloudless blue as the kids toss in bed. The air conditioner runs and offsets an otherwise early morning calm. The pool is empty.

Yesterday the kids swam alongside other hotel guests. Midday everyone ran for cover, for shade. I sat poolside in the gazebo for eleven hours. After breakfast I sat and read through early parts of this book initially titled Lots of Birthdays.

I visited with a person in the gazebo next to us. She too is from Oregon. She drove the night before from Salem. She works in corrections with the youth population. "It's scary what their normal includes," she says.

In other words they are not celebrating twelfth birthdays poolside in the central California sun. Madeline wanted this for her July first birthday celebration. Now that is two days away.

They sleep on the pullout couch. There is a second bed in the bedroom yet they prefer to spend their time in the studio part of the hotel room. They too overlook the pool palm trees and blue sky.

Later we will have breakfast and then swim for an hour. Then we will drive to the outlet mall. There's a Chili's nearby and Madeline remembers this restaurant as well. We ate there while in Las Vegas last July. It was hot there too.

Steaming hot, stopping most outside activity. My wife noted yesterday the heat reminds her a bit of Scottsdale. Still she thinks Scottsdale might have been cooler than this near record Sacramento heat.

I needed a nail clipper last night. "My luggage is drenched," said Abby. In other words good luck looking in there for anything specific. We sort through her duffel and find the clippers early on. Last week I watered the front yard and swept the driveway.

Reaching down for broken glass I hit my thumbnail on the broom handle; the handle top with its solid plastic cap. It slices my thumbnail and stops our mid morning cleanup routine. Madeline runs for a band-aid. Days later the remaining nail needs to be clipped. Still I keep a band-aid on the raw thumbnail area and avoid the pool.

I watch from poolside as they dunk their heads and swim. They join in a pool of activity. I read from inside the gazebo. Its orange canvas shields the sun and allows any breeze to pass through.

I read through two hundred fifty handwritten pages. It recaps a Lake Tahoe spring break, my oldest brother's surprise Vermont birthday party and our ongoing daily routine.

A daily routine which includes: kids tossing in bed, and air conditioner noise. The everyday which is backdrop to the new activities while on vacation. The new sights, sounds and invariably outfits, and shoes we find along the way. This too, keeps luggage drenched.

I watch Madeline swim in the pool below. A large black bird flies from palm tree to palm tree. It lands at the second story window level. I watch Madeline swim; I watch the raven secure its perch.

There is not a cloud in the central California sky. Just then I realize I didn't get my morning writing done before heading off to breakfast. I write a few pages as Melissa and the kids enjoy the pool. Our friend Lynn flew in last night to join us for a day in Reno and a twelfth birthday party poolside tomorrow.

The news continues, dominated by the Jackson family affairs. Meanwhile today Farrah Fawcett is laid to rest after a Los Angeles cathedral funeral. Abby helps spread suntan lotion before adults join Madeline in the pool.

Yesterday I gave two copies of my book to strangers sitting poolside. One I'd visited with a day earlier. She will place it in the juvenile detention facility library. They too can benefit from listening to life, or at a minimum read about this notion. Ideally they implement it and are able to leave the detention center one day.

Not sure where the other copy will land. They spoke with a southern accent and maybe my book will let them relive parts of their vacation to the California capital. I wrote part of it while poolside in Sacramento last fall. They will also read about Oregon, Portland and Bend, one of the five fastest growing regions of the country at the time I wrote my first book.

It's fun to read of places familiar. It's fun to watch from a hotel window as people read our books down below poolside. What do they think as they read along?

Are we successful in placing them in our settings? Do we bring them back to the California sun, even while they sit poolside, reading within this same setting? Do we stop them long enough to think of their own life, to listen in on their life?

We write daily of the everyday. Sometimes it's the passing of celebrities, other times watching the rippling pool below, or enjoy seeing palm trees which line the pool and much of California landscape.

Later we will drive to Reno. We will have a buffet dinner and watch a few Circus Circus acts. Ideally I'll sit and play blackjack as well. Reno should be ten degrees cooler than the near one hundred degrees of Sacramento.

The kids have the pool to themselves this morning. Sunday there were nearly thirty in the pool. Not standing room, yet not allowing for open swimming either. The air conditioner works even in the early morning hours.

Two kids and their mom join them in the pool. The kids with the cute sunhats we saw at breakfast. Melissa dips her toes in the pool and returns to her shaded gazebo. The kids swim from side to side with their goggles.

"Watch this!" they said yesterday as they swam and dunked their selves often using one hand to hold their nose. It slows their swimming pace. Abby just took a dunk as she holds her nose. The sunhats are now in the pool too. They linger on the pool steps.

I swam yesterday morning and will join them tonight. Later I will copy a few financial pages from the business center computers. Today is the last day of the second quarter and will see if change is noted on our financial schedules. Mid year and many wait for better days ahead.

We write daily and sometimes it's mid morning before reminded there is writing to do. Writing to log in the everyday and those days spent poolside in the California sun. For some it is our last day of being age eleven.

Today I am in the hotel business center looking at the end of second quarter numbers. Down forty six point nine six percent reads a government statement. Our PIP, or personal investment performance according to the government website for federal employee retirement accounts.

I also look at the publisher's website. They note traffic to their website, specific traffic for my book on listening. They also track sales. Four are listed since its publication and release the end of April 2009.

I sit in the hotel business center and fill in my three pages of early morning writing. Later we will have breakfast and swim. Mid afternoon we will have birthday cake and celebrate Madeline's first dozen years.

I also go online to check airfares. I was told years ago to never prepay. Still with many reservations and travel plans, prepaying sometimes secures bargains. Other times last minute fares hold cheaper rates. Today I look for flight, hotel and car rentals for my nephew's July wedding in Vermont.

We delayed reservations hoping there would be cheaper fares later on. We look for bargains when investment accounts lose forty seven percent in one year no less. This recession continues.

The hotel lobby fills with people starting their day with complimentary breakfast. Then they swim, lounge or see the sights in and around Sacramento. We drive to Reno and return via Lake Tahoe. We enjoy mountain vistas and setting sun along the route. Lake Tahoe glistens around the curves of Zephyr Cove and later Sacramento ahead as the sun colors western sky.

We had a buffet dinner at The Eldorado before leaving. They have counters full of food: Asian, Mexican and American. We fill with meats, salads and desserts. The gelato is a treat. The kimchi - a surprise. It'd been years since having this Korean spiced cabbage dish while serving overseas.

I played blackjack after seeing one show at Circus Circus. A young oriental girl twirled an umbrella. Later she holds five umbrellas with her feet. We are entertained. The kids, Melissa and friend stay for two more shows. A woman on a rope climbs, dangles, and amuses. The third show is Diablo.

I am up early as I sit and play blackjack and later walk a bit of downtown Reno. I leave with twenty two dollars and fifty cents which offsets part of this vacation. I see the group having breakfast. It's time to join them; join them and share our end of the second quarter numbers. Change is delivered.

Chapter 32

I'm back in the hotel business center. I'll check e-mail one last time before we drive home later this morning. First we'll have breakfast and swim awhile. Early morning and late afternoon the weather is perfect; midday not so much. The clear skies keep us indoors or sweating in the cabanas.

Yesterday I read more of web economics. The different ventures started. Some last, others peter out early on. Some try introducing internet based currency. Others try using fractional money, in other words three cents for this, several more pennies for that.

People look forward to bargains yet know early on when shortchanged. Still the internet is here to stay. Those who develop a website or presence early online often have the advantage.

Today's world becomes smaller and more interconnected with each passing day, with each additional internet connection. We no longer need a market place. Goods don't need to be stored, transported and warehoused. Instead we meet in market space - a global market space.

Goods are sold via the internet. Already over a third of United States' products are purchased from buyers overseas. They can order from their terminal and then the goods, services or information is sent to them. A virtual market space which covers more of the world, regardless where we sit in ours.

Today this is the central California sun. Madeline celebrated her twelfth birthday poolside and with a dinner along the

American River in Old Town Sacramento. We were early as the restaurant serves dinner at five pm.

Thus we sit, watch boat traffic and shield ourselves from the sun, Shades keep the sun at bay and allows whatever breeze to cool the restaurant. There are also overhead fans doing their best to circulate the record heat.

Today we will drive back to Oregon. It's no doubt ten degrees cooler ten hours north. The breakfast crowd fills the hotel courtyard and atrium. We've eaten here several times now. The business center has three terminals. One is used behind me as a woman occasionally types a few words, amid the clicking of her mouse. I'll join her once these morning pages are written.

We write poolside, during breakfast or waiting to log on to hotel computers. Melissa just stopped in to ask if I ate breakfast. They will grab something to eat and then lounge by the pool before we pack and head home for Fourth of July celebrations; the Fourth of July and a neighbor's surprise sixtieth birthday party. Meanwhile California issues IOU's. They too struggle in this economy or lack of economic activity.

The first day back from vacation, there is a list of things to catch up on: mail, yard work, research airfares and send off an RSVP. There is a surprise birthday party later tonight as a former neighbor turns sixty years old.

When he celebrated his high school reunion, I'd made a mental note he is the age of my oldest sister. Just now I realize I made the association based on year of high school graduation. Thus he is my oldest brother's age, although my neighbor graduated in 1968 which corresponds with my sister.

I'll look through paperwork and clear up more month and quarter end business details. It's early morning the luggage rests where we dropped it at midnight. Everyone sleeps in after a long drive back from Sacramento.

We were delayed as they wanted one more swim. We checked out at noon, along with much of Sacramento. The traffic is snarled midday because of a motorcycle wreck.

Later we miss the Interstate 5 entrance and follow a circular route through Marysville and Chico before rejoining the interstate near Red Bluff. We got a late start and then delay because of traffic and secondary roads. At Redding we find a familiar Olive Garden and the now too familiar one hundred seven degree heat.

We sat poolside in Sacramento and enjoyed a day trip to the Reno, Lake Tahoe area. Today I'll catch up from being away several days. The calendar turned while away. There are chores outside and business details inside. I drove through several neighborhoods within Rancho Cordova. Some are well kept and surprised there aren't any for sale signs.

Speaking to a local resident while at a grocery store, he reminds me there is a whole community up for sale just across the boulevard. He longs to live elsewhere; Reno or maybe Utah as he tires of California. "They haven't sold the family farm back in Ireland," he muses.

Sometimes it's difficult to know what to do next. Clearly California with its current financial crisis has many residents looking for Plan B, or perhaps Place B. Their place in the sun is too costly, so they look elsewhere for cheaper places; places with more clouds.

For much of the week it is clear skies, thus the heat. Portland too has a heat wave. Still I'm happy to see the lawn withstood several days without water. I reseeded before leaving and some of it takes. I'll mow, water and continue the yard work cycle. Today is a catch up day after a quick vacation to the California sun.

It's July Fourth. Already a few have given a lightshow. Tonight there will be more inside the planned park community fireworks and those from the surrounding neighborhood. Those illegal fireworks compete with the city's show.

Last night our former next door neighbor had a surprise sixtieth birthday party. He is speechless as he walks into the hall. There is food, music and fun. The second surprise sixtieth birthday party in as many months.

Melissa finishes preparing potato and fruit salads. We will watch fireworks from a neighbor's deck. They have as good a view instead of joining crowds at the community park. Today is near record heat once again. It's hot for much of the country. I made reservations yesterday for the Vermont July wedding. Waiting until the last minute often secures good rates.

Not so much this time. Maybe people travel to Vermont for a midsummer getaway. It will be hot there too. The wedding is outdoors beside Lake Champlain. The reception indoors in Burlington, also overlooks this lake.

Birds sing outside my den window. The kids sleep in after a night of movies and pizza with a friend. We saw our former next door neighbors once again. We've met at restaurants on occasion, otherwise they live in a different community. One they hope continues to grow with shops, theatres and restaurants. A pedestrian friendly neighborhood which struggles to materialize in this economy.

Still if it is meant to be it will develop. The area next to the airport was in development for many years, being stalled by events of nine eleven. Today there are shops, restaurants and even Ikea.

An airplane makes its way across the sky. I'm late in writing, although being on vacation last week, there wasn't routine to my morning writing or even the rest of the day. Vacation, a time to leave schedule behind seeing new people, places and activity.

Ideally we leave with new perspective. We see our world with new focus. Last night was a reminder how people enjoy life and take time to celebrate the milestones.

A surprise party works for some, others are frightened by the idea. Still someone has to do behind the scenes planning. Last night the party continued on its own. People dance as the band plays. The full moon at one end of the manicured yard, setting sun at the other. A late evening breeze keeps it perfect for outdoor activity.

The retractable wall of glass opens the reception hall to the outside. Several note this setting could be Hawaii. For some it is just this, an aloha moment as they toast in the new decade. A sixth decade of life, celebrated among family, friends, and neighbors.

The July Fourth fireworks are over. There are as many this year. Before and after the community lightshow others display theirs, some louder and nearer. The one hundred degree heat keeps many indoors until late in the evening.

We barbecue hotdogs and hamburgers. Eat salads - potato, pistachio and five cup fruit. Then we have chocolate cake. There are twelve candles atop as we celebrate Madeline's birthday a second time.

The first cake we ate in Sacramento, although not the chocolate with white frosting ordered. The baker must have been inundated with holiday and wedding cake orders. Madeline fills in for an altar server this morning. Midday yesterday they call to see whether she would be available. Some out of town on vacation, others perhaps up late celebrating the Fourth of July and missing early church services.

Today is cooler. I'll go for a walk as the past few days have been near record heat. It's hot even in the shade. I cut back some of the mimosa tree as it continues to branch out. It now covers a smaller section of our back patio.

I shopped for replacement trees yesterday. The December ice storm leaves a few in bad shape. We will replace several trees once we return from this July vacation. "How long a vacation?" Abby asks. "Are we going to rent a car?" She thinks we are going for a birthday party. It's a trip back east for a nephew's wedding.

It's been planned awhile although we waited until last minute to make reservations hoping prices would come down. People still travel apparently as prices hold. Madeline received several cards and more iTunes for her iPod. She still saves for her computer. They continue to come down in price as technology improves.

Governor Palin steps down from running Alaska later this month and this starts a conversation with America. Many wonder her next move. She is watched by supporters and arguably watched closer by her detractors. They don't like she plays her own tune. She is a pioneer blazing new political trails. Still much of the media concentrates on a Hollywood death a week earlier.

Other celebrities have since passed on yet one continues front and center. We celebrate surprise sixtieth birthday parties yet he doesn't live beyond age fifty. Some are more famous once they pass on, their income streams grow with their now even more infamous stature. History has a few larger than life figures, while others manage this while alive.

The Fourth of July fireworks are done for this year. The summer heat has let up. Today there is no blue sky, clouds keep it cooler. We spent much of last night outside. Our patio not used as often as brochures for patio furniture would have us believe. We ate take out Chinese with neighbors.

A dice game, Farkle, followed. Then dessert before going inside as the summer heat disappeared. Now the kids sleep in after a weekend of Fourth of July activity. We celebrated a former neighbor's sixtieth birthday and then watched fireworks the following evening.

Now it's back to beginning of the week routine. I'll water and hope for the return of our front lawn strip. Brown spots continue, even with the additional watering and reseeding. It takes awhile for it to rebound.

Many spent their weekend at the beach. Traffic to and from the coast is a slow drive. The birds sing outside as there are more birds this time of year. Our neighbor noticed them last night wondering where they go in the off season, or even during the recent heat wave? They find shade like the rest of us.

We hope for sunshine and then it becomes too warm so we find the shade of a tree or gazebo. Sacramento poolside meant being in a cabana. There was a breeze yet canvas kept the sun at bay.

A neighbor is coming over later today. She plans to motivate the kids to clean their space, their bedrooms, and the family room. She plans to help them organize and start a system which keeps them on schedule.

Cleaning like anything else is easier if we stay with a plan. Start with a plan. The hard part is continuing with that plan. We don't follow through daily, weekly - ongoing.

Those who do, have lives which mirror this commitment. More happens in their lives. They make room for it, literally if not figuratively. They rid of the old and make room for newness to enter. Their life flows rather than clogs with hoarding.

There are the school projects, the extra pairs of shoes, and shirts. There is the abundance of technological gadgets and teddy bears. Today stuffed animals go by various names and descriptions, still they move off store shelves with increasing frequency.

From the store shelves they land in a kid's room, family room, crowding our home's space. It fills nooks and crannies, overtaking living space. We forget space is a commodity.

We fill life with stuff, insulating and crowding our surroundings. We are affected by what we view daily. Sometimes it's necessary to throw out our accumulation of subscriptions, newspapers, and travel mementos. Those we take in hope of reading or at a minimum reviewing. The brochures, knick knacks, the stuff which later crowds work space, family and living rooms.

Today is overcast. As good as any day to sort through, purging, making room for newness to come in. We take it one room, stuffed animal, one memory at a time.

Our neighbor just left for work. Soon her sister will ring our doorbell. Then the kids will spring into action, cleaning, sorting and organizing their space; living spaces burdened with stuff. Stuff once important, becomes less so with the passage of time.

Yesterday a friend celebrated a birthday. She shares her birthday with Nancy Reagan and the most recent President Bush. We will meet for a Mexican dinner and exchange a few gifts. A staple is Sees Chocolate. It's the surprise gift which is harder to find. Madeline will make a card.

They both sleep in after a day of cleaning. Our neighbor had them motivated to clear their spaces. Some went in the garbage, some to Goodwill. Still other stuff finds its way into their bedroom closet, dresser or on their desk.

Ongoing stuff crosses our lives. Sometimes it moves to its proper location, other times stopping midway, cluttering view if not space.

Today I'll call the doctor's office. Abby now has ear trouble. She doesn't like going to the doctor yet her ear is not clearing up. We hoped it was from days spent in the pool and maybe the water pressure caused her discomfort.

It's quiet outside early morning midweek. It's overcast again yet no rain is expected. A few showers would help the vegetation. Sacramento was in bloom, contrasted with the areas which weren't watered daily, those areas parched a golden wheat.

The beach book signing is a month away. An author I'd met awhile back e-mailed the bookstore announcement. She wonders if I knew there was a book signing planned in Lincoln City. She met me for coffee months ago as I had questions on the business end of writing.

She was one of the authors at a local mall book signing. I wanted to learn more of the book business. How to market and track ongoing sales? She has ideas, one of which was this beach bookstore. She also says to open a separate bank account as this is a simple way to track sales activity. Still she warns not to expect huge sales early on, or even later.

Write for the love of writing. Write for ourselves. Find satisfaction there and hope later others enjoy our thoughts penned in daily. Our activities logged in daily. Our life recorded ongoing. Our life and the life of others we come in contact with.

Our neighbor crosses the street to motivate our daughters to clean and organize their rooms. A skill they will use each day going forward.

Being organized, putting stuff away keeps life flowing and helps those who follow behind. Sorting through our own stuff is time consuming. More so sorting through debris left behind from others: the winter tires, broken Christmas tree, the garage sale finds of years past.

"Get rid of the Christmas cards," says our neighbor. They are in a cardholder on the dining room bookshelf. We no longer see them. She does. It is now July and says to get rid of them. She says this often as she goes room to room. She has an eye for design. Still the first step is in finding the room behind Christmas stuff found in July.

Today I'll plant a new tree. The peegee hydrangea doesn't survive last year's snow and ice storm. I'll replace it with a dwarf white royal magnolia. This is the plan as I sit writing an hour behind schedule.

I sorted through 2002 paperwork. The receipt from the temporary storage unit which held our stuff as we moved house. The hotel receipts for the weeks we spent across state as my mother in law battled cancer in a nearby care facility.

2007 had its own share of paperwork ready to discard. Bank statements and travel receipts. I cleaned some of my den as the kids played with their stuffed animals and later played on their Hawaiian mandolins. I took a break and join them with a guitar I'd bought for Christmas. If practice makes perfect, this was the first session and it didn't go well.

Last night a neighbor called to tell us another neighbor had passed away. He had been swimming earlier and never left the changing room. Frank would be ninety one this month. Still it is a surprise as he walked often and seemed fit like someone decades younger.

We were celebrating another friends seventy third birthday across town when someone came by with the news. Instead they continue on to our next door neighbors with news of Frank's passing. An airplane climbs in the sky, another overcast morning. Laundry whirls from across the house. The dishwasher works too. Yesterday Madeline and Abby made deviled eggs.

I started the day intending to make pancakes. There isn't enough batter after adding blueberries. I add an egg and milk.

Finding a ready made cornbread mix, I add it in and stir it together and then bake it a half hour. The kids eat it later, surprised they enjoy what started as pancakes with too little batter.

This morning they sleep in. Melissa too. She was awake two nights ago as Abby didn't sleep, complaining of an earache. The swimming pool and record heat might add to her ear trouble.

They swam often while on vacation. They are now sleeping in, resting for our next trip midmonth. Travel is always an adventure. We are taking an overnight flight east via Phoenix. We return via Atlanta. Seems a circular route to bucolic Vermont, yet this is the route with lowest airfare.

I also throw out records of past frequent flier mile schedules. The most recent records are online and thus no need to keep stacks of this along with records of medical appointments, insurance receipts years later.

I read through a letter from someone who has since passed. We'd sent her a gift for her birthday. She wrote a six page thank you. She mentions her health, ideal computer configuration and the everyday. She too writes of her life.

We write our life story over and over is how someone succinctly phrased it years ago. True even for those who've since passed on. They continue in their letters of their morning routine. For Frank this included a few laps in the community pool, however not this morning or going forward.

A garbage truck drives along the loop. I just put out this week's garbage, recycling and yard debris. Yesterday I planted a new tree; a dwarf white royal magnolia replacing the peegee hydrangea. I will wait to replace more once we return from vacation in Vermont.

The kids are excited about the overnight flight. They took one to Newark, New Jersey a few years ago. As they get older, those overnight flight schedules will become less appealing.

Then again, there is a sense of saved time as we sleep and travel overnight. Often we sleep once getting to our destination. We allow an extra day before the activities begin. First a family get together, then a wedding and later a brunch followed by another family get together along the shores of Lake Champlain.

I look online for advice on lawn brown spots. Some recommend aerating; get the aerating sandals, it lets the ground breathe. Others disagree. Still the curbside lawn strip is not turning green regardless of my additional watering, reseeding and even higher mowing.

Maybe it's the slope of the grass strip. Perhaps the sun reflects from surrounding pavement. Another website states it might be too much water. Most likely it's a combination of neighborly pets and the extra walking, tracking through winter and early spring.

The lawn and garden shops are busy as I walk through in search of a royal star white magnolia. Some enjoy their free time gardening. Suppose for those with a green thumb, it has more appeal - reward. Our neighbor who motivated Madeline and Abby to clean watered a few indoor plants while she helped dust and clean our family room.

I later water them before my daughters note they'd been watered earlier in the day. Maybe the lawn too receives an over watering. It's a chore, not so much the joy of gardening as a store advertisement claims.

Melissa ran errands after having a family dinner at the Spaghetti Factory. She returns with a garden hose complete with nozzle. Our backyard hose broke recently. Sun damage cuts the hose in half.

"Water often," advises the store salesperson as he gives me a bargain on a tree they've had in inventory awhile. His mom says to give it to me free if they find one. In other words it's off season for this species. We find one. Not in the healthiest condition, yet alive assures the son.

I leave with my car size bargain and throw out the mere tree trunk left from the peegee hydrangea. It doesn't survive this past winter's record snow with a mix of ten days of ice. Rime, while pretty with its reflection harms nature. Most break under the additional weight of a cover of ice.

Someone should invent a lighter time released rime which waters plants as the reflective ice melts. Whatever rids grass of brown spots works for me. So far nothing has.

An airplane crosses the sky. Coffee brews as the kids sleep in midsummer. I aerated the yard yesterday. After driving the Volkswagen through the Department of Environmental Quality emissions test, I stop at a local department store for aerating sandals.

They also have containers of earthworms. I heard on the radio they too rid lawns of brown spots. They are Nature's own tillers. They work the soil as they move about, burrowing air pockets as they go.

I also cut back the butterfly bush. The whole plant is going in the recycle bin as it is now considered an invasive species. Clearly they are one of the easiest plants to grow.

They've shielded the air conditioner well. I'll look for some other shrub to cover the air conditioner. The computer search says to use ornamental grasses.

Allow a three foot buffer between the unit to provide repairmen access. The coffee pot beeps. I've a few more pages to write, before coffee and beginning the morning outdoor routine. This means watering, even in the often drenched Pacific Northwest.

I checked the publisher's website to see activity on my first book. The web page is in the process of upgrading. It's fun to see the number of hits. Also Googling, I find my book listed in Italian. The internet translates our world into a smaller, more connected world community.

The internet keeps us in contact. Still this past week several United States and South Korean computer databases are compromised. Some use criminal approaches to their computer time. Ideally they serve jail time for this opportunistic criminal activity.

The world wide web makes the world accessible to the small operator. It keeps the world connected and in contact with each other. Facebook, Twitter and other social media forums have some questioning the merits of the virtual community. Another group watches television, perhaps a mass hypnosis. Another year of Big Brother began last night. Some less enthused by television programming, or lack of program, written script.

Another airplane flies by. Two days ago Interstate 84 was closed due to a liquid asphalt spill. Today there is a barge lodged at the bottom of the Columbia at Hood River. There's trouble moving through the only sea level pass within the Cascade Mountains.

Later we will have dinner at a restaurant across town, across the state line. Dinner in Washington state with friends. The setting frames Mount St Helens and Mount Hood. The Columbia River floats down below as airplanes approach or depart Portland's airport. We will be in this air traffic in less than two weeks.

We are excited for the trip to Vermont. My nephew will marry mid July along the shores of Lake Champlain. Abby looks forward to the overnight flight. Another airplane passes by.

The morning newspaper waits in the driveway. The front page has a picture of a free flowing Columbia at Hood River. Yesterday a barge had grounded there with its heavy load of oil. The day before Interstate 84 was closed due to an overturned eighteen-wheeler. The interstate leading east out of Portland parallels the Columbia River for miles.

Last night we sat along the river as we ate hamburgers, or fish and chips. The locally based restaurant also operates a brewery. They have several brews ready to order and experiment with. Traffic across the Columbia River on Friday night is experiment enough.

Melissa leaves directly from work and has a corner table waiting. The folding glass panels open the outdoors as river traffic passes below. There are sailboats. People walk the promenade. Airplanes take off and land at PDX just across the river. Today our friend will be in this air traffic as she flies back home to London via the nonstop Portland to Amsterdam flight.

I spent much of yesterday inputting revisions on the computer. "Oh," says Madeline "so you took the first paragraph and dispersed it among the first few chapters." This after telling her I reworked the opening pages to *A Sibling Within*. I deleted twelve pages in the process.

We keep more readers with each word removed. I read this awhile back and wondered the validity of this observation. Still we know when to edit sentences, or even whole paragraphs which don't add to story.

Last night we enjoyed dinner with friends. First they came over to use the computer to print a boarding pass. The seat selection process often is made at the last minute. Perhaps this is a remnant of nine eleven. We booked our flight to Vermont online yet parts of the route are not available for advanced seat selection.

Suppose this is fine for those traveling alone, not so good for families with young children who prefer to sit as a group. I print a fresh copy of my second book. It contains perhaps ten revisions, thus it's been awhile since printing a new working copy. Now I'll edit yet again and hope to send it to the publishing house soon.

I began writing this twenty years ago. Some parts lived back then, other parts date back thirty years. Still we spend current day formatting words to paint the picture, place the reader beside us in settings that matter; people within those settings that matter.

An airplane flies overhead. Our friend left for London yesterday. The first flight is cancelled due to mechanical problems. The alternate route takes her nonstop Seattle to Heathrow. Travel is an adventure, often not going as planned.

I walked to a Starbucks yesterday. Once while at the beach Madeline noted it was like walking on a postcard. The ocean setting took her away with its beauty. Yesterday I took the wooded trail to the neighborhood coffee shop. I too wanted to place myself in a postcard setting.

The trail ends in a nearby park. The park with the winding sidewalk is the cover of my book on listening to life and taking it from there. I sat at a picnic table and took in this setting.

It isn't a postcard rather inspiration for my first book. The front cover along with a summary on the back helps market books. Story keeps them reading, yet we need a handle to place books in the buying publics hand.

A neighbor three houses down the street passed away last week. We sent him a birthday card for his ninetieth last year. He responded with thank you written in ten languages. The kids and Melissa often rolled down the car window when passing his home and yelled, "Hi, Frank." Invariably he would smile and wave back.

I included two pages on him in my first book. We write of people who people our lives. We write of the everyday including the climbing airplanes, surprise sixtieth birthday parties and friends who finally reschedule their flight out of town.

It's early Sunday morning. A drizzle falls as birds sing outside my den window. Yesterday I continued on to the mall without a Starbucks coffee. Instead we used a coupon for a restaurant meal at the mall. The coupon expired yesterday and thus Melissa and the kids met me for dinner. I later walk back home taking a circular route.

I walk past established neighborhoods and others stopped mid construction. The light rail made its first trip last week to the nearby mall. Now we can travel to the airport in twenty minutes, downtown in forty using light rail - the Green Line.

This should boost business in this corridor southeast of downtown. It may also reignite development, a planned village stopped two years ago due to the down economy. Still more shops, restaurants and a luxury hotel are planned.

There will be even closer coffee shops and retail stores. It's nice being in a neighborhood within walking distance to business. For the past six years we've driven errands.

This works on days of drizzle or the more frequent rains of the Pacific Northwest winter and spring. Still during the summer we water yards and vegetation. Another airplane flies by.

Today I have a list to get through. I will renew my drivers license. They require those turning fifty years or older to have eye exams, along with a new photograph. I renewed the Department of Environmental Quality certificate midweek last week.

Madeline wants a library card. I want the local library to keep longer hours. Opening at midday seems short hours and not convenient for those who read during their summer vacation.

Abby will come along and I hope leave with a card of her own. They sleep as the rains of yesterday continue this morning. That's ideal for the magnolia purchased recently. I'll replace the tree outside the family room window and one to cover the air conditioner. Maybe both will be palm trees as they are available more often at the nurseries lately.

Palm trees in the Pacific Northwest would seem out of place yet many yards have the otherwise tropical plant. I read through ten pages of *A Sibling Within*. The opening pages to a book begun long ago. It's finally coming together. There is a beginning, middle and end.

Writing should include all three, even though many stories start in the middle. They begin in the middle and go from there. We write ongoing yet like a painting which stops somewhere interesting, words too stop or at least end on the book's last page. Then it's up to future readers to take the story further.

Bestsellers are furthered by word of mouth. Whether placed in brick and mortar stores or rely on the internet, books are marketed best word of mouth. A good story is passed on.

I walked back from the mall restaurant the other day. Midsummer, a perfect time to spend outside. Today it rains. Water tables enjoy the rare summer rain.

Next week we leave for my nephew's wedding in Vermont. They have a website devoted to their special day. There is a write up of how they met, details of the marriage ceremony and a gift registry. There are also photographs and a guest book.

We had dinner along the Columbia River this past weekend. Soon we will celebrate along Lake Champlain. The sixth Great

Lake some refer to this lake which separates New York from Vermont.

The body of water which separates the Adirondacks from the Green Mountains. It also connects Burlington to the Atlantic via the Hudson River, and to the Great Lakes via the St Lawrence Seaway.

Water still vital to everyday and long term health. Marriage, too, if all goes well. Water available as backdrop as we write, eat and celebrate weddings and family surprise sixtieth birthdays, amid the everyday of life.

Other times we celebrate overlooking the Pacific. A wind gust moves the shrubs and berry bushes. Several smaller birds fly alongside a lone seagull. Yesterday there were hundreds as we had lunch at Kyllos restaurant overlooking the Oregon coast.

Sun shadows play on the north side of our deck. The seagull flies past once again. We will have a late breakfast at a nearby casino. First I'll complete three pages and then take a walk along the ocean. Melissa and the kids sleep in, as Abby grunts and shifts in her sleep.

"We are on the back of the ocean," said Abby. There's no sand in sight. Her postcard day at the beach includes sand - beachfront. Instead we overlook vegetation, several two story homes, and the ocean a half mile away. We will be back for a book signing for Northwest authors later this summer.

Before then we will travel to Vermont for a nephew's wedding. I hope they, like the gourmet food bookstore manager, can help me find something. Readers perhaps - those who enjoy celebrating surprise birthday parties and those who appreciate smiles on the May page.